Prince William County & Manassas

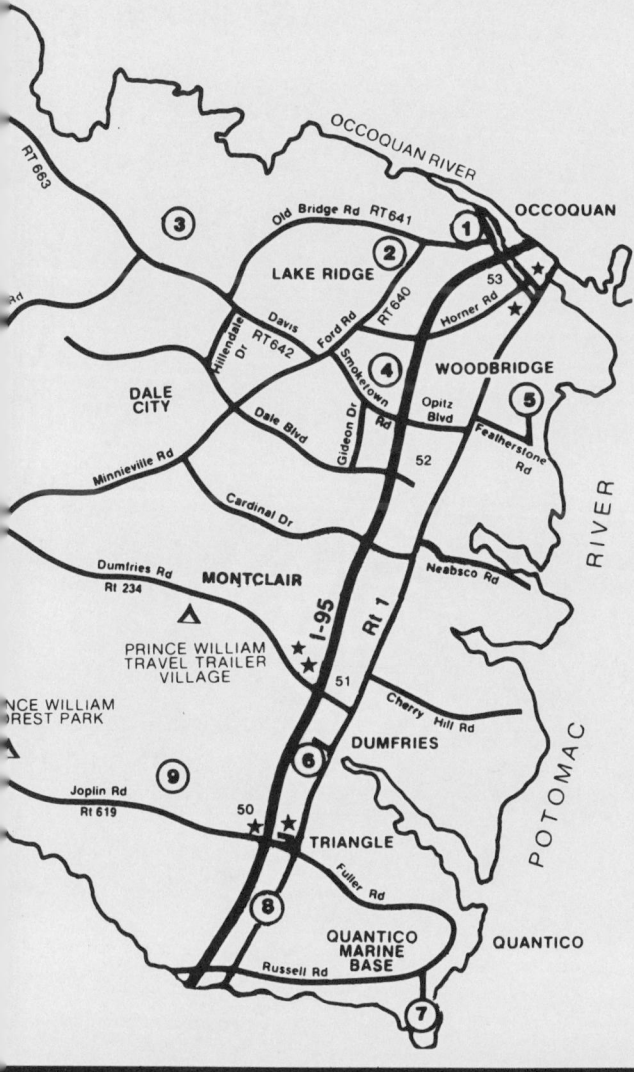

8 **Locust Shade Park:** Bumper boats, pedal boats, mini-golf, batting cages, concession, and driving range.

9 **Prince William Forest Park:** Hiking, fishing, orienteering, group and family camping.

10 **Fairground:** Northern Virginia's largest argricultural exposition in August. Other special events.

11 **Old Dominion Speedway:** Weekend drag and stock car racing. Top NASCAR drivers.

12 **Manassas Hills Golf Course:** (9-hole par 3)

13 **Old Town Manassas:** Walking tour includes Manassas City Museum, Antique Car Museum, restaurants, and shops. Exit 11 (I-66)

14 **Ben Lomond Park:** Pool, waterslide, bumper boats, mini-golf, racquetball, and tennis. Civil War reenactment in August.

15 **Hayloft Dinner Theatre.** Professional dinner theatre features musicals and comedies. Exit 11 (I-66)

16 **Manassas National Battlefield Park:** Walking and driving tours. Electric map and slide show explain major battles fought on these grounds. Exit 11 (I-66)

17 **Prince William Golf Course:** (18-hole par 70)

The following pages contain highlights from the pictorial history of

*Prince William County, Virginia
created out of Stafford County in 1731 and named for
Prince William Augustus, Duke of Cumberland,
second surviving son of King George II of England.*

At the time Prince William began, its population was spread over the present-day counties of Prince William, Fairfax, Loudoun, Arlington, part of Fauquier, and the city of Alexandria. In fact, Prince William County was almost synonymous with Northern Virginia as we know it today. That was over two centuries ago, however. This history deals with Prince William County in the boundaries it enjoys in 1988.

Prince William County

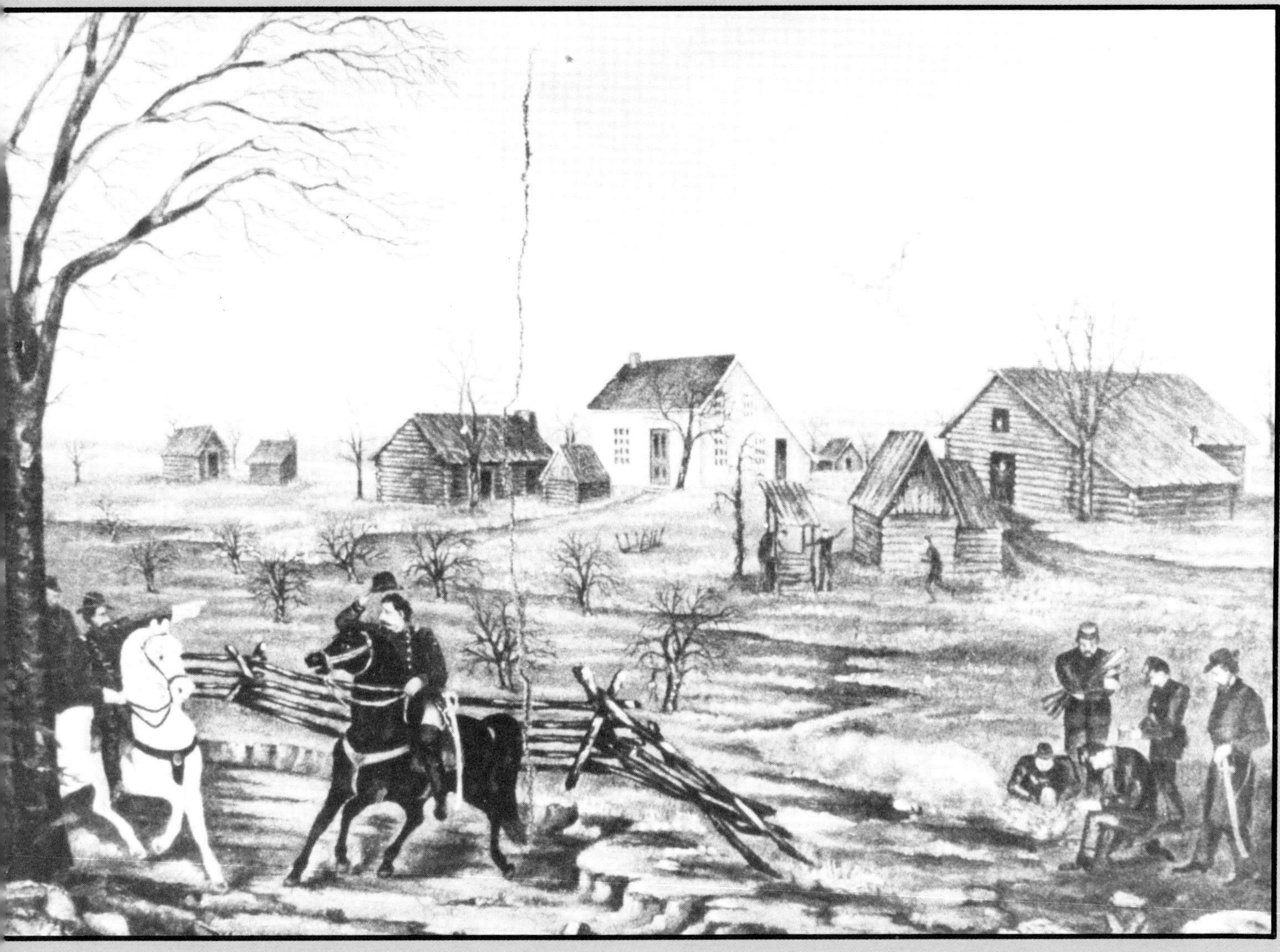

A Pictorial History
By D'Anne Evans

Copyright © 1989 by D'Anne Evans

All rights reserved, including the right to reproduce this work in any form whatsoever without permission in writing from the publisher, except for brief passages in connection with a review. For information, write:

>The Donning Company/Publishers
>5659 Virginia Beach Boulevard
>Norfolk, Virginia 23502

Edited by Christina Cramer
Elizabeth B. Bobbitt, Senior Associate Editor
Richard A. Horwege, Senior Editor

Library of Congress Cataloging-in-Publication Data:

Evans, D'Anne A.
  Prince William County : a pictorial history /
    by D'Anne Evans.
    p.   cm.
  Bibliography: p.
  Includes index.
  ISBN 0-89865-772-5
  1. Prince William County (Va.)—History—Pictorial works.
2. Prince William County (Va.)—Description and travel-Views.
I. Title.
F232.P86E88   1989   89-1305
                                                    CIP

Printed in the United States of America

Contents

County Seal 1

Acknowledgments 7

Chapter 1
   The Earliest Days 9

Chapter 2
   An Urban Landing for the River Trade 13

Chapter 3
   A Time of Division 21

Chapter 4
   Along the River and the Railroad 35

Chapter 5
   Gateway to a New Century 47

Chapter 6
   Part 1 Marines Settle on the Long Water 67
   Part 2 Pre-World War II Prince William 75
   Part 3 Greenwich 85
   Part 4 As the Past Serves the Present 91

Chapter 7
   Part 1 A New Deal for Prince William—
          Chopawamsic RDA 103
   Part 2 Transition Time 111
   Part 3 Wartime in the Forest 117
   Part 4 After the War 121

Chapter 8
   Part 1 Prince William Faces the Future 129
   Part 2 How the City Reached Prince William 141

Chapter Notes 170

Bibliography 172

Index 174

About the Author 176

Acknowledgments

About eighteen years ago, before I had any idea of writing about Prince William County myself, I had the good fortune to come across a guide to Prince William County as it was in 1941, written by local historians and financed by the Works Progress Administration of the New Deal years. It is known locally as "People and Places," which is really very appropriate. The people and places of Prince William County in 1988 have proved every bit as fascinating as those written about in 1941. In that respect we should note, not only the people, but the places have changed somewhat.

I have many people to thank, because in the short time allotted for preparation of this book, I had to draw heavily on the research, writing, and recollections of others. I need also to reiterate that this is not meant to be a definitive history in the academic sense of the word. It is intended to be a look at the past in pictures, most of which have not been published elsewhere.

It is hard to know where to begin, but first thanks ought to be given to Edith Moore Sprouse, whose extensive files on Prince William County provided a solid research foundation. Thanks also to Lois Loehr Brown, former special education supervisor for the county, who offered books and memories.

The Prince William County Historical Commission has provided constant, friendly help. Members to whom go special thanks are: Chairman Jane MacDonald, former Chairman Don Curtis, James Cooke, Marie Caton, Lucy Phinney, Margaret Callander, Rose Hazel, and Tom Nelson. Staff members who went out of their way to be helpful were Don Wilson of the Central Library, County Archaeologist Jan Townsend, and Planner Mavis Stanfield. Director of Tourism Bernadette Plunkett was very helpful, as were Nicholas Carosi and Linda St. John of the Chamber of Commerce. County Supervisor Ed King was generous with time and advice. At the County Office of Economic Development my thanks to John Gessaman and Maureen Hannan.

In Dumfries my special thanks to Barbara Kirby, Ann Hoagland of the Dumfries Museum, Town Historian Lee Lansing, Hilary "Pete" Costello for the explanatory tour of his home, "Williams Ordinary," Donna Swanson of the Dumfries Mini-Library, and Clarence Woodward, Andrew Collier and Ellis Hawkins of the Possum Point Power Station.

Supt. Jim Klakowicz and Chief Ranger Mark Schuppin at Leesylvania State Park went out of their way to provide information, as did Director Doug Harvey, Elsa Lohman Shirmer, Dave Purschwitz, Celeste Lopina, and Mrs. Lewis Carper at the Manassas Museum.

From the staffs of the two National Parks in Prince William, outstanding cooperation came from Ranger Historians Barbara Burchette, Barbara Maynes, and Jacque Lavelle at Prince William Forest Park, and from Historian Ed Rauss and Ranger Historian Jim Burgess at Manassas National Battlefield Park. In Washington, I had the good fortune to deal with Marine Corps Archivist J. Michael Miller, Curator Dick Long, Assistant Archivist Paul Hallam and Volunteer James Pilkington at the Marine Corps Museum; with John E. Taylor, Larry McDonald and Volunteer Tom Wyatt of the Modern Military Records Division at the National Archives, and with Dr. Kenneth McDonald at the CIA.

At the Potomac High School Library, repository for the James Haynes Collection, friendly assistance was given by Jean Galladet, Vivian Ivy, and Jean Dunovan.

Those who helped me find information and gave generously of their time and family records also include Althea Hooff Cooksey, Janna Lee Murphy Leepson, Martha Joynt Kumar, Evelyn Ognowski, Marianna Durst, and, at Linton Hall, Sister Anita Sherwood, O.S.B.

To all those who took time out to be interviewed and have shared their family records, many thanks. Most of these are listed for recognition in the Oral History section of the bibliography, but to any whose names were left out, my apologies. This year spent learning about and writing about Prince William County has been one of the most rewarding in a long life.

D'Anne Evans
Burke, Virginia

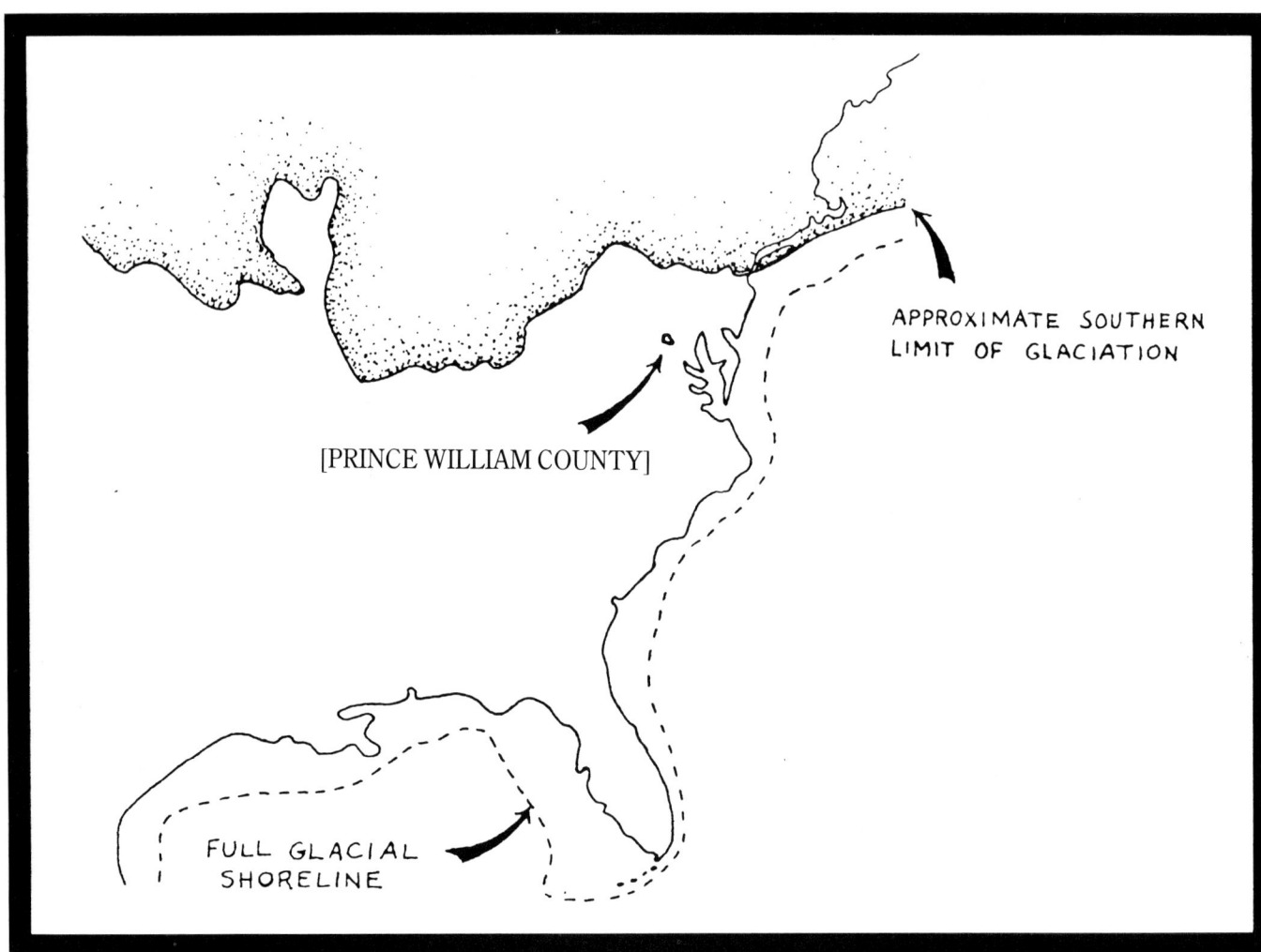

*The coastline of the eastern United States was very different eleven thousand years ago and before, because there were glaciers to the north. As the glaciers melted over thousands of years, releasing millions of cubic feet of water, the coastline was flooded. There could be settlements of major importance from the Archaic Period (8,000 to 750 B.C.) and before, buried in the bottoms of rivers, creeks, and the Chesapeake Bay itself.
Map courtesy of Michael F. Johnson*

CHAPTER 1
THE EARLIEST DAYS

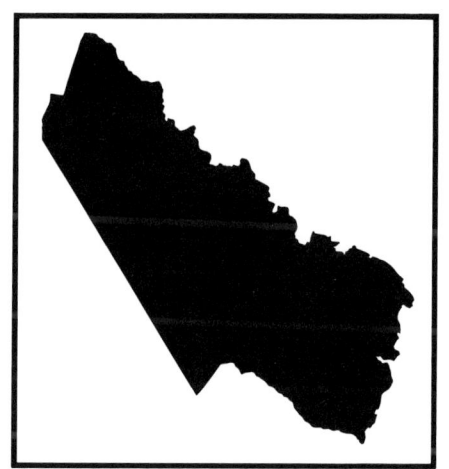

Because of its geographic location and attendant circumstances, Prince William County has usually been on the trailing edge of development and growth in the surrounding region. In colonial times, the core of settlement was at Jamestown, moving outward to the north, south, and west from that point. Just over a century and a half later, by the establishment of the federal city of Washington, Prince William's magnetic focus shifted to the north. Instead of being a satellite of the government at Williamsburg, and later Richmond, people in Prince William, willing or not, were drawn inevitably into the orbit of their ever more numerous neighbors to the north. Now, in the latter half of this century, the county is part of greater metropolitan Washington.

PRE-HISTORIC PROSPECT

Archaeologists theorize that land above water in Prince William today served only as sites of outlying hunting camps of the Paleo-Indians who came to the area in about 9,000 to 9,500 B.C. The Paleo-Indians' major settlements are now probably underwater, or in an area we can no longer excavate. Their centers have literally "gone under," according to Fairfax County archaeologist Michael Johnson.[1]

Much more evidence exists to acquaint us with the Indian culture existing at the "Point of Contact," the arrival of the English settlers. Some of the conclusions drawn by the first explorers and the scholars who read what they wrote is being reinterpreted today. The Algonquin tribes who lived along the Potomac may not have been as primitive in their cultural development as previously supposed. National Park Service Regional Archaeologist Dr. Stephen Potter believes, on the basis of research he and others have done, that the Algonquins were on the verge of blossoming into a complex political structure when they were interrupted by the coming of the English.[3]

In 1607, when Capt. John Smith first explored the Potomac to the fall line, there were differences in the landscape in what is now the political division of Prince William County. At that time the creeks that cut their way down to the Potomac were deep and wide. The Occoquan, the Neabsco, the Yosocomico (later Powell's), the Quantico, and the Chopawamsic bordered wooded, hilly peninsulas of picturesque beauty. Indian villages were situated on the shores at good fishing spots. They were inhabited by Algonquin tribes of the Powhatan Confederacy at the times of seasonal hunting and fishing, such as the run of herring in the spring or the fall migrations of waterfowl. Most of the year these tribes had important permanent settlements elsewhere. The assessments of the Algonquin culture, based on the Potomac fishing camps, is like basing an evaluation of American civilizations on a look at a beach or ski resort, rather than at our industrial cities.

Inland, on the savannahs of western Prince William, lived the Manahoac, encountered by Captain Argall in 1613.[4] It was not they who were the principal threat to expanding settlement, however. The Manahoac were pressured not only by English intrusion from the south, but by the warlike Iroquois of New York state, who were in the process of making Virginia their hunting preserve as they had done with much of central Pennsylvania.

The meandering mountains, stretching from north to south, served as a guideline for two powerful groups, first the Susquehannocks of Pennsylvania in the seventeenth century, who were replaced by their conquerors, the Iroquois of New York, and the Cherokees and Catawbas of the Carolinas. Every spring these adversaries put on their war paint and set off in search of each other. The tribes who lived along the way were often their unwilling hosts to save their own skins. Other Indian tribes and the English sought to use each other as buffers from the predatory travelers of the Great Warriors' Path. By 1669, the Manahoac had disappeared as a tribe, their hunting grounds appropriated by the Iroquois.[5]

THE FLASHPOINT

The English were equally determined to have this new Iroquois preserve for their own, however, and were harder to drive out than the Manahoac had been. They were, moreover, not merely watching out for Indian expansion: they had an eye out for the advance of their centuries' old adversaries, the French, as well. As the Council and Burgesses informed the Crown in a petition drawn up in 1720, they wanted to "secure our present settlements from the incursions of savage Indians" and also of the "more dangerous French Incroachments."

Northern Virginia was a hazardous place to live for over a century after the landing at Jamestown. It was not until after 1722 that substantial numbers of people were persuaded to settle in the area.

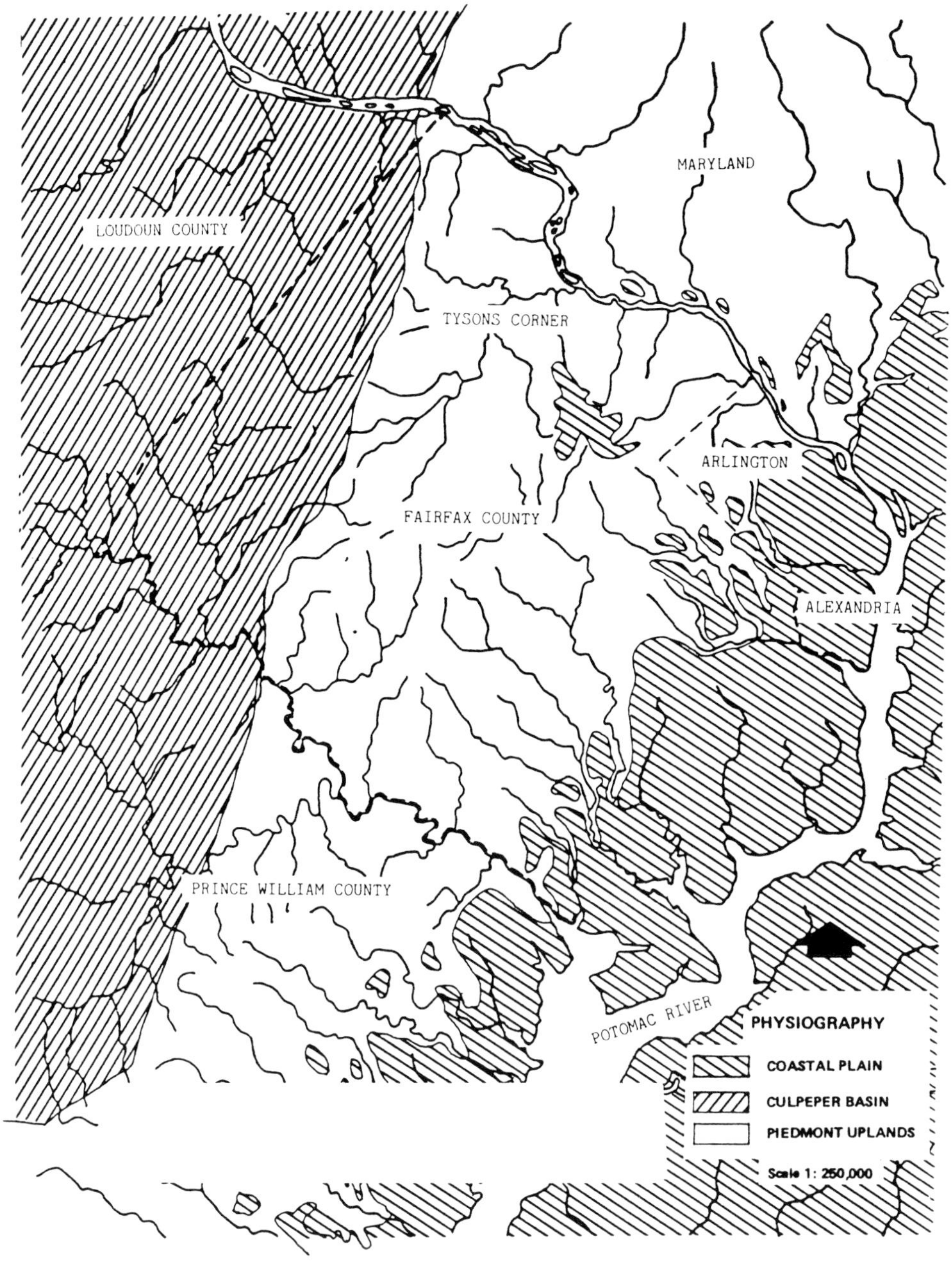

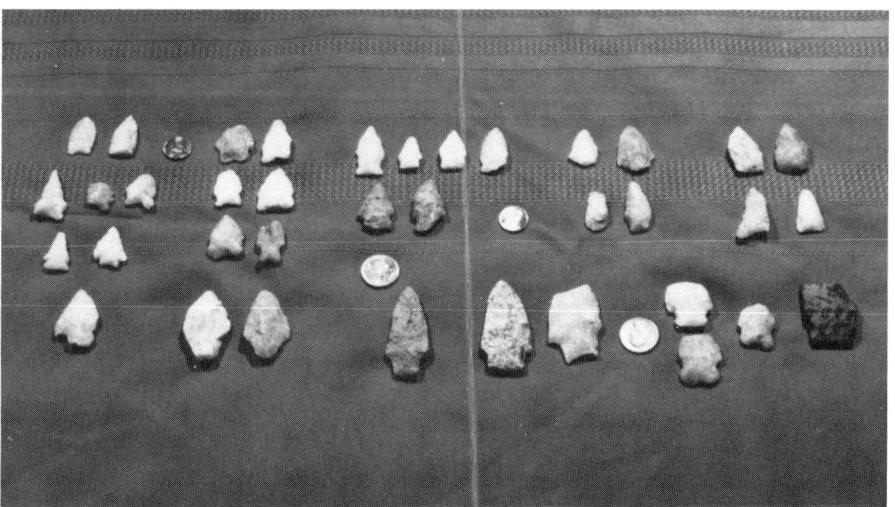

Only a few professional archaeologists have done studies in Prince William. More has been done in neighboring Fairfax County, a part of the same region. In both cases, the workers have found campsites and artifacts of prehistoric people, but they do not regard them as definitive. Almost uniformly, archaeologists agree that much of the evidence that would tell us of these long ago people is underwater, under concrete, or plowed under. These "points," as stone weapons and tools are termed by archaeologists, were found over a period of years on a farm in southern Prince William County. The majority are attributed to Indians who lived about 3,000 B.C. A very few could be dated as far back as 7,000 B.C.[2]
Map courtesy of Michael F. Johnson

Bel Air ∞ Prince William County, Virginia

This is Bel Air, one of Prince William's earliest plantation homes. Might it have begun as a fort, after the clashes between Indians and white settlers in 1675 and 1677? The colonial government's first effort to protect the outlying settlers was to order a fort built on Neabsco Creek in 1679. Because the provision for the four forts in the Virginia statutes are vague, other than that they be on the rivers, there is room for debate on where they actually were. They may have been inland, away from tidewater, so the soldiers could observe the movements of the Susquehannocks. Another local place would have been where the Neabsco crossed the Potomac Path, a major north-south travel route for the Indians. Bel Air's lower story measures roughly sixty by twenty feet, the specifications set out for the fort buildings. There is general agreement the building could have been used as a place to keep prisoners being taken to court, whether it was built for that reason or merely used for that purpose later. Shackles were found attached to the wall in the room called the donjon. The exact location of the fort was not documented, but several clues exist to suggest it may have been on the site of Bel Air, better known as the home of the Ewell family and Parson Weems. The ground floor has several characteristics of a seventeenth-century fort, for example, the two-foot thick walls, the wine cellar or donjon, the massive fireplace, and the fact that the walls only go a short distance into the ground, with no footings to bear additional weight of other stories. This suggests a hastily erected building, which may have had an additional wooden superstructure. Evidence also exists of a possible series of stockades enclosing the building, all later abandoned in favor of a more flexible defense plan.[5]

Courtesy of Edith Sprouse collection

CHAPTER 2
AN URBAN LANDING FOR THE RIVER TRADE

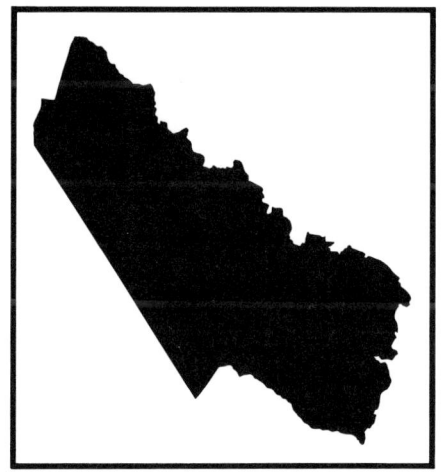

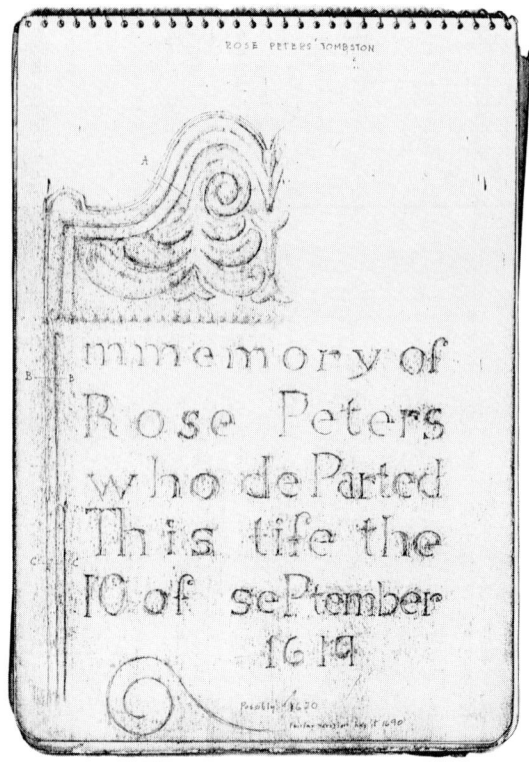 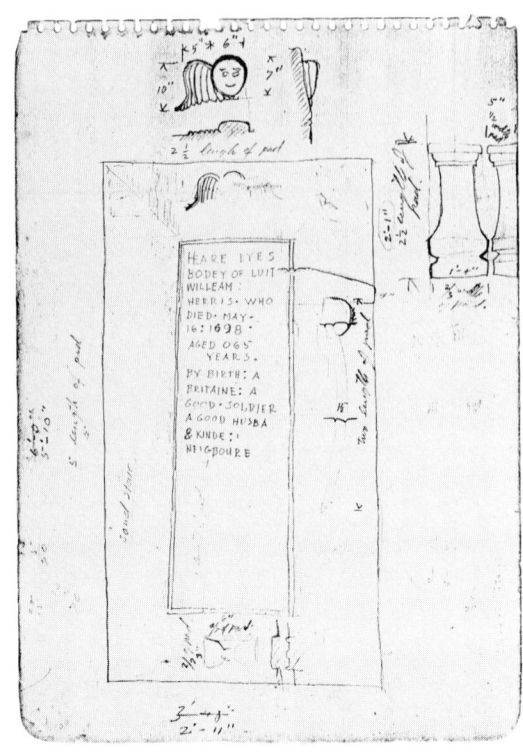

The policy, first of the London Company and later of the Crown and the Lord Proprietor, was to induce as many British subjects as possible to come to the New World to stay and, by occupation to secure Virginia as an English possession. This proved to be a more hazardous and expensive business than any of them had anticipated.

Disappointed that gold and silver such as the Spaniards had acquired in the conquest of Mexico and Peru were lacking farther north, the first Englishmen in Virginia had a consolation prize—the green gold of tobacco. Their efforts to mine this leafy mother lode were the focus of colonial affairs.

The new settlers at Jamestown naturally secured the land near their settlement first. Plantations at a distance from the seat of government were less desirable. Nonetheless, there were still petitioners when the land nearby was gone, so patents were issued for the distant areas. In 1653 the first patent was issued for land in present-day Prince William County, although at that time the location was not called Prince William County.[1]

A few intrepid landowners began to move to their isolated holdings. They hadn't been there long when, in 1675, Indian uprisings began. This caused many to return closer to the southern settlement until the situation stabilized. Not until 1722, when the Indians agreed to stay west of the Blue Ridge Mountains, under terms of the Treaty of Albany, did settlers come back north in large numbers.

In marketing their crops and buying manufactured goods from home, the Virginia planters dealt mainly with English merchants. England did nost exclude outside competition quite so rigidly as did the Spanish, but they, like other nations at the time, had a protectionist system. Even Scottish merchants from Glasgow, who undertook to build a trading position for themselves in Virginia operated under heavy restriction. The Scots practiced various stratagems to avoid the requirement that American exports be carried only in English ships only to English ports and that only merchants legally defined as Englishmen could carry on trade in the colonies.

Then in 1707 the kingdoms of England and Scotland were united, and the restrictions on the Scots were lifted. They had already captured a substantial share of the Virginia tobacco trade for sale in France and Europe. After 1707 they were able to set up stores where they stocked goods for colonial consumption. Those who traded with the Scots did not have to send orders to London for goods. They could buy on the spot.[2]

In 1730 mandatory inspection of tobacco ready for export went into effect. Padding hogsheads of tobacco with sweepings from the barns had become all too common a practice as early as 1710, when Gov. Alexander Spotswood arrived. Although he tried almost immediately to institute regulation, it was not until 1730 that a tobacco inspection law was passed in Virginia to which the London authorities also assented. It was this requirement that all tobacco be brought to a central inspection point that laid the formation for the foundation of towns.

In 1749 the town of Dumfries was chartered by the legislature, another triumph for the Scottish representatives of Glasgow firms. They had convinced the reluctant planters that business could be transacted more efficiently in towns. This was a turning point in the general aversion to urban development that had existed in Virginia from its early days. The trustees for the town of Dumfries as organized in 1749 were John Graham, Peter Hedgman, William Fitzhugh, George Mason, Joseph Blackwell, Richard Blackburn, and Thomas Harrison.[3]

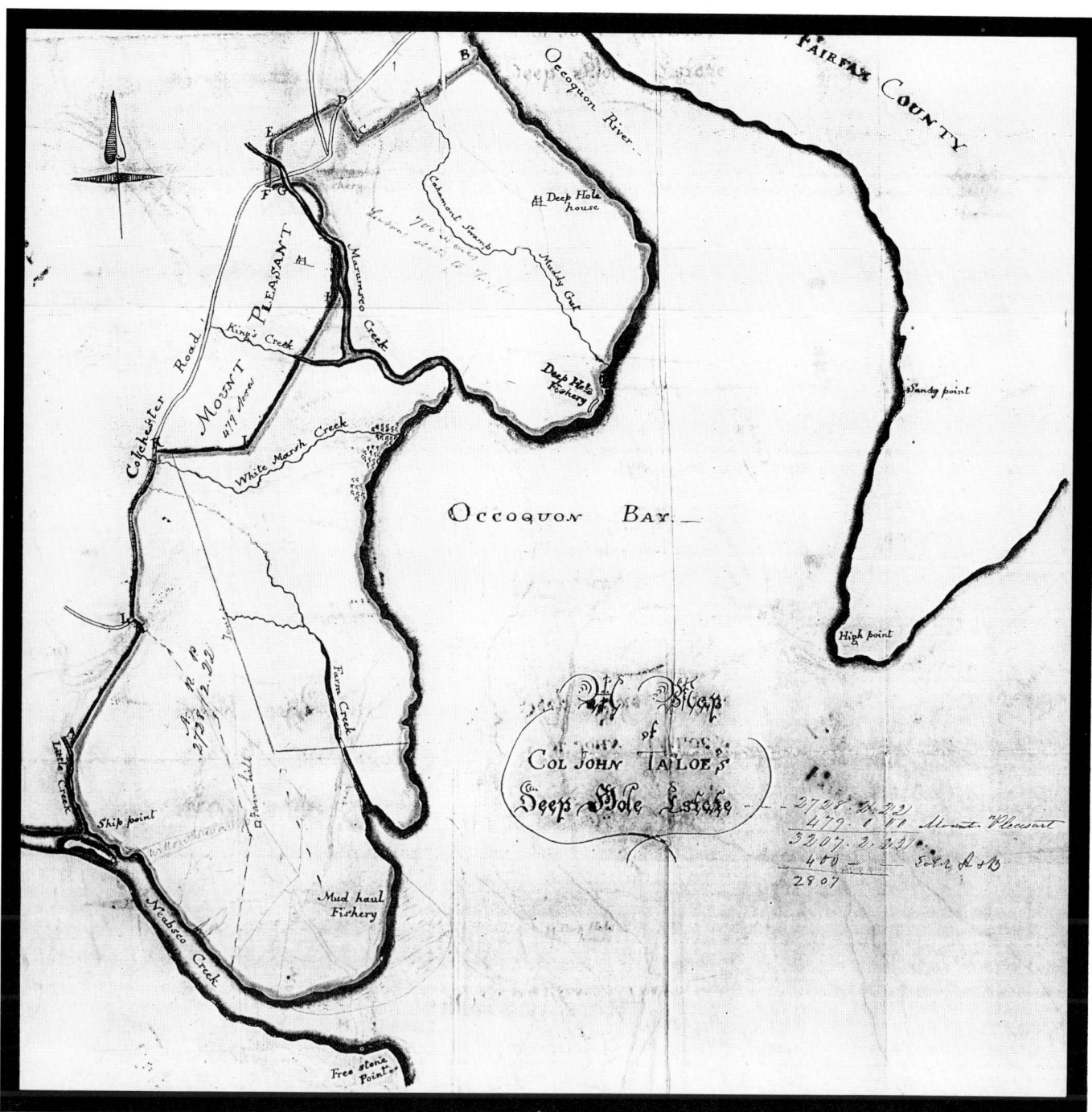

Not many people were living in this area, the 1988 border between Prince William and Fairfax counties, after the Indian uprisings of 1675 through 1677. Even late seventeenth-century gravestones are scarce. James Haynes sketched these markers for Rose Peters and William Herris before they had to be moved out of the path of Interstate 95. One inhabitant, whose grave was found and of whom more is known, was Martin Scarlet, a prior owner of Colonel Tayloe's "Deep Hole" plantation. Scarlet was a member of the house of burgesses. For several years, starting in 1682, Scarlet assisted his neighbor, Col. George Mason, who had been ordered to provide ferry service across the Occoquan for the patrol of twenty rangers protecting the area against Indian attack. Col. John Tayloe, who acquired Deep Hole Plantation in the eighteenth century, also owned land on Neabsco Creek, where he operated an iron foundry.[4]

Map courtesy of the Virginia Historical Society; drawings courtesy Katherine Haynes

> To Severall p^{rs}. Intended for y^e. West Indies
>
> To Peter Peyret Minister, his wife, two Children & two men to goe to New Jersey .... £ 50.
>
> To Peter Lesade Ploughman, his wife & 2 Children ... 3£.
>
> To Lewis Reynaud of Angoumois, his wife & Eight Children for tools & other Necessaries things to goe to virginia .... 8£.
>
> To Nicklas hayward Notary for y^e. Passage to virginia of Lewis Reynaud, Anne his wife, francis, Lewis Mary & Sara Reynaud their Children & Benjamin Reynaud Mary his wife, Marianne & Mary their Children & John de la Raumette .... 33£.
>
> To y^e. Same Nicklas hayward for y^e. Passage to virginia of Michel Maury, Marquis Calmes Peter Ribotteau & John Neyrac .... 12£.
>
> To Lewis Reynaud & his family for Supply .... 2£.
>
> £ 108.

In 1686 and 1687 four men obtained a large grant on the southwestern boundaries of Prince William, intending to accomplish several objectives. One was to provide recently arrived Huguenot refugees with land of their own and religious freedom, guaranteed by the King of England. In return, the former French families would safeguard the frontier and keep an eye on the Indians passing north and south along the Carolina Road, at the foot of the Blue Ridge Mountains. Sturdy homes would be needed in that perilous terrain. Some Huguenots did take up residence in what was called the Brent Town Tract. Every so often, in an old house in the area, an architect with an eye for historic detail spots some indication this may have been built around the core of a very old house, perhaps a fortified one. The kitchen fireplace pictured here suggested to the restoration architect that the core of this eighteenth-century home in the Brent Town Tract, may have been seventeenth-century. Genealogist Don Wilson came across this passenger list of a ship that sailed for Virginia in 1687. On board were several French families known to have been among the early settlers on the Brent Town Tract, their passage paid by Nicholas Hayward. When Fairfax Harrison wrote Landmarks of Old Prince William, *neither this manifest nor the survey of the Brent Town Tract, now in the University of Virginia library, had been found. Harrison therefore assumed no one had settled there.*[6]
Courtesy of the author

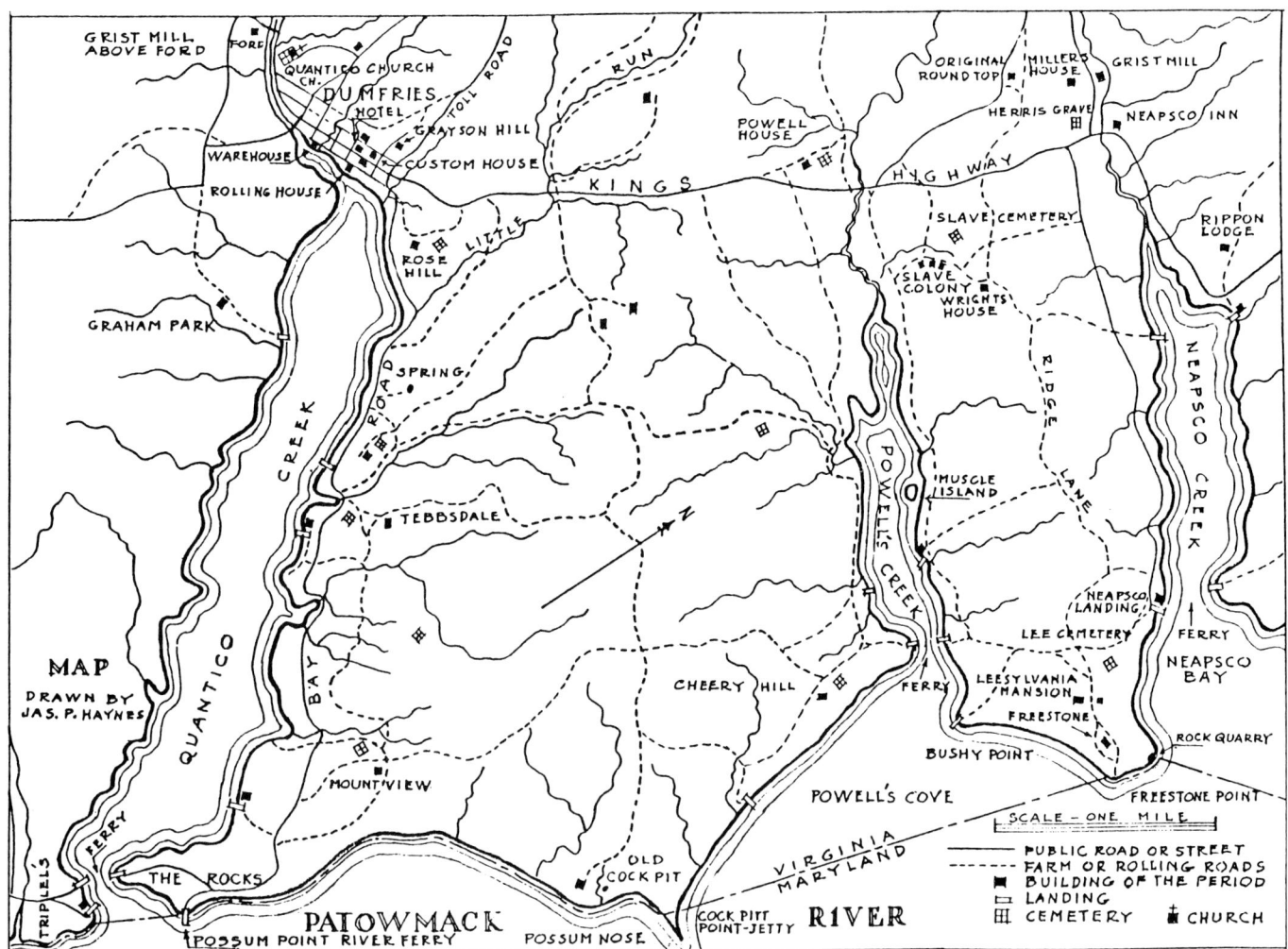

All along the riverfront in Prince William County, where the broad, placid creeks join the probing surge of the tidewater Potomac, lie the ruins of colonial plantations. Very few grantees had come up to claim their land before 1722, the year Governor Spotswood journeyed to Albany, New York, to conclude a treaty with the Iroquois. By the Treaty of Albany, the men of the Long House agreed to stay west of the Blue Ridge. Heartened by that news, the settlers streamed into the northern reaches of the Old Dominion. Demand for tobacco was at its peak, and every possible acre was planted with the big cash crop of that era.

Unfortunately the wooded, hilly peninsulas of land along the river did not prove suitable for tobacco cultivation nor for other row crops. Over the years the people went elsewhere, and the forest took its own back. It took a history enthusiast with the energy and interest to explore the territory and consult the deed books in the county archives to find the landmarks of two hundred or more years ago. James P. Haynes worked as an architect for the federal government in 1949, when he moved his family to a house on the edge of Cherry Hill peninsula with a view out over the water. Every weekend he and one of his sons hiked around the area exploring. He also did a survey on a large scale showing how the port of Dumfries silted up. This can be seen at the Weems Botts-House Museum in Dumfries.

Map drawn by James P. Haynes, courtesy of Katherine Haynes

HILLSIDE FRONT

RIVERSIDE FRONT
FREESTONE
AS RECONSTRUCTED

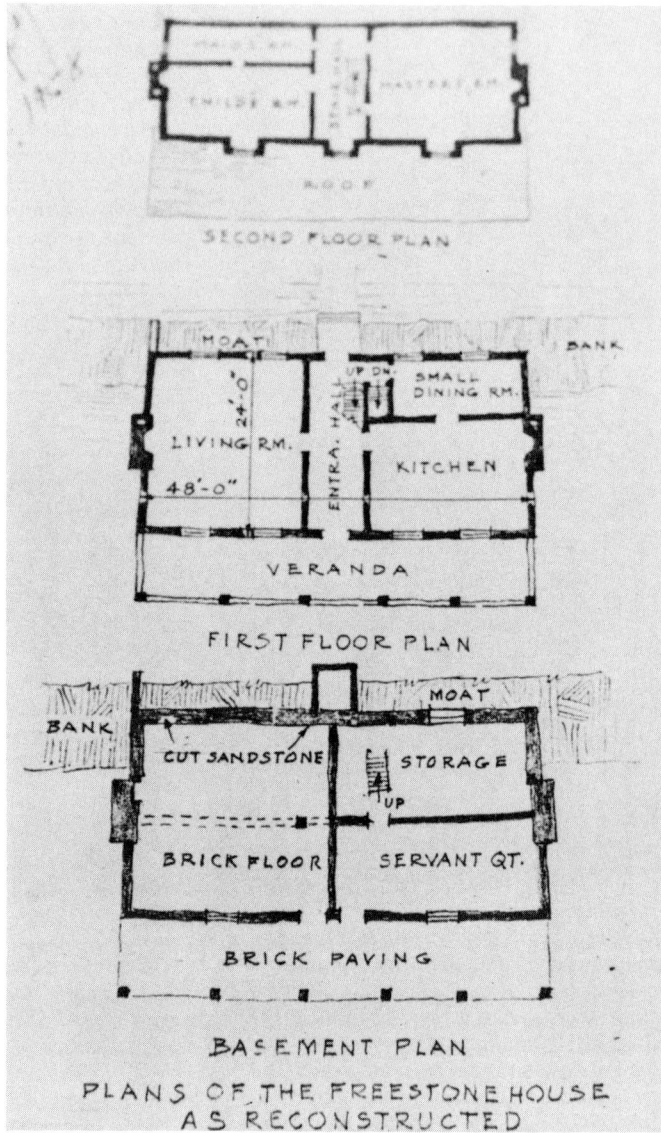

PLANS OF THE FREESTONE HOUSE
AS RECONSTRUCTED

*Of all the sites marked on the Haynes map of his plantation exploration in mid-twentieth century, only Rippon Lodge survives in recognizable form. However, at the time Haynes was exploring in the 1950s, there lived in the area a very old woman named Wigglesworth, who had been born and spent her childhood in what was then called "the surveyor's house." It is also called the Fairfax House, for the nineteenth-century resident owners. From her description, Haynes, with his architect's training, was able to give us a picture of the house that sat just below the brow of the hill.[7] Tradition has it that Henry Lee II and his bride, Lucy Grymes Lee, lived in the surveyor's house on their arrival at Leesylvania in 1754, while their house at the top of the hill was being finished. This would indicate that the surveyor's house may have been the house used by the Lee overseer, the "quarter," a token compliance with the legal grantee's obligation to establish a settlement.[8]
Courtesy of Katherine Haynes*

Shown here is a photo of mapmaker-architect James Haynes, taken at Great Falls, 1930.
Courtesy of Katherine Haynes

This frontispiece, drawn by James Haynes for his unpublished novel Belle of Leesylvania, *illustrates a situation typical of plantation business before 1730: the ship calling at a riverside plantation dock for its consignment of tobacco. English merchants deplored the extra turnaround time this created for their ships. They would have liked a one-stop trip at a supply point, but they blocked urban settlements which would have cut into their business by creating a concentration of artisans to serve the planters' needs in Virginia.*
Courtesy of Katherine Haynes

What ultimately broke the economic pattern of isolated settlement and brought about urban development is represented by this small building, the tobacco inspector's office at Dumfries, which stood until 1971. After 1730, no shipment was accepted that did not have an inspection certificate. The certificates could be used to pay taxes, to trade for goods with merchants, in other words to lift Virginia out of what was mostly a primitive economy.[10]

Although Dumfries was not officially chartered as a town until 1749, some believe the nucleus of a town was there earlier. Dumfries town historian, Lee Lansing, noted certain typical seventeenth-century architectural features of the tobacco office suggesting construction prior to the inspection act of 1730. Governor Spotswood's Tobacco Inspection Act of 1713, which was disallowed, provided for the establishment of three agents' houses. Two were in present-day Stafford County. The logical place for the third would have been on the Quantico at the site of the colonial port. There is no firm evidence that it was there, but the tombstone of William Dunlop, the agent of a Glasgow merchant, was found on the Quantico at Dumfries.[11]
Courtesy of the Weems-Botts Museum

The zenith of Dumfries' meteoric rise as a tobacco port came about 1763, when its tonnage of shipping reported was greater than that of New York. It takes some exercise of the imagination to see the handsome Georgian building in the picture as it was then. It was called Williams' Ordinary and stood beside the main north-south route, the "Potomac Path," awaiting stagecoach visitors or the carriages of such luminaries as George Mason or George Washington, come to attend a ball, or the theatre, or the races. George Mason, on his way back from Williamsburg, may have been stopping here in 1774 when he formulated the first of those objections to British policy voiced by Virginians. "The Prince William Resolves" of June 6, 1774, were the first of a series of protests against the erosion of colonial liberties. Next in the series came the Loudoun Resolves and the Fairfax Resolves. Mason added the proviso that citizens should boycott British goods if their liberties were not given better protection.[12]
Courtesy of Hilary Costello

In the days when young John Davis tutored the Ellicott children, the family home, built by John Ballendine about 1758 and called "Rockledge," was one of the few homes in Occoquan. Davis wrote that the aspiring industrialist had failed to induce settlers to come. Although ships sailed up the river to load cargos of flour, "Occoquan consists only of a house built on a rock, three others on the riverside, and half a dozen log-huts scattered at some distance."[9]
Courtesy of the Library of Congress, Historic American Buildings Survey, Virginia

CHAPTER 3
A TIME OF DIVISION

In this letter from "Light Horse Harry" Lee to his father, Henry Lee at Leesylvania, written from New York in 1786, the young officer expresses his concern that his house in Dumfries had better be repaired lest it fall down, making him a resident of Dumfries as well as Leesylvania. Printed by permission of the Virginia Historical Society

Thomas Jefferson wrote of his home state in 1781: "We have no towns of any consequence...the *laws* have said there shall be towns but *nature* has said there shall not, and they remain unworthy of enumeration." The census takers of 1790 did not entirely agree with Jefferson—they considered Richmond, Alexandria, Norfolk, and Petersburg as towns in Virginia worth counting.

If the census had been taken twenty years earlier, they undoubtedly would have included Dumfries, Prince William County's promising port of entry. By 1790, however, the ship channel on Quantico Creek had silted up, and the population in the west of the county was growing instead.[1]

Other population clusters began to appear at strategic geographic spots. Several were chartered by the legislature: Buckland in 1798, Haymarket in 1799, Occoquan in 1804 and Brentsville in 1822. Buckland was named for the architect who designed and built the home of Samuel Love. He was the same William Buckland who built Gunston Hall for George Mason. Before Buckland Hall was built, it is said the little group of homes near the mill on Broad Run was called Deer Lick.[2]

Haymarket had grown up around a tavern at the junction of the Carolina Road and the road from Dumfries across the mountains to Winchester. For a brief period, from 1803 through 1807, Haymarket enjoyed a time of prominence as the home of the district court for the four counties of Prince William, Fauquier, Fairfax, and Loudoun.

Even while the port declined, the gentlemen justices of the county court met in Dumfries, bringing with them the business attendant upon "court days." The courthouse had been relocated from Cedar Run to Dumfries after the formation of Fauquier County in 1759. However, even before the port ceased to function, rumblings of discontent had begun. Courthouses were supposed to be equally accessible to all citizens and were usually located in the geographic center of a county. Dumfries, on the river boundary at the eastern end of Prince William, was an exception. Citizens living on the western perimeter made known their opinion of this situation in a petition sent to Richmond in 1779. They wrote: "Governor Fauquier, for reasons best known to himself, fix(ed) the Court of (Prince William County) at the Town of Dumfries, a part of the Cou(nty) inconvenient to at least three fourths of the inhabitants thereof...."[3] This undeniable inequity was eventually addressed in 1820 by creating the new town of Brentsville in the center of the county and moving the court to it.

Although for Dumfries the hour in the economic limelight was brief, it should also be remembered as the home of some outstanding citizens of the early republic. They include: governor of Virginia and Revolutionary War hero "Light Horse Harry" Lee; one of Virginia's first two United States senators, William Grayson; the fifth commandant of the U.S. Marine Corps, Archibald Henderson; and George

Several years after Lee wrote, this unprepossessing little building on the old road from Dumfries to the mountains became the center of a thriving trade down the southern coast. In what is now the Weems-Botts Museum was the office and bookstore of the Rev. Mason Locke Weems, an itinerant bookseller, who was also a clergyman. A young Englishman, one of the first tourists in the new republic, left an interesting word picture of Mr. Weems. At the time he met Weems, John Davis was earning money to continue his travels by tutoring the children of Nathaniel Ellicott, owner of the gristmills at Occoquan. Wrote Davis:

"About eight miles from the Occoquan mills is a house of worship called Powheek Church.... Hither I rode on Sundays and joined the congregation of Parson Wems, a Minister of the Episcopal persuasion, who was cheerful in his mien that he might win men to religion... the discourse of Parson Wems calmed every perturbation; for he preached the great doctrines of salvation, as one who had experienced their power.... Of the congregation of Powheek Church, about one half was composed of white people, and the other of negroes. Among many of the negroes were to be discovered the most satisfying evidences of sincere piety.... After church I made my salutations to Parson Wems, and having turned the discourse to divine worship, I asked him his opinion of the piety of the blacks. 'Sir,' said he, 'no people in this country prize the Sabbath more seriously than the trampled-upon negroes. They are swift to hear; they seem to hear as for their lives.... Oh! it is sweet preaching, when people are desirous of hearing! Sweet feeding the flock of Christ, when they have so good an appetite.'

"'How, Sir did you like my preaching?' 'Sir,' cried I, 'it was a sermon to pull down the proud, and humble the haughty.... Sir, you spoke home to sinners. You knocked at the door of their hearts.'

'I grant that,' said Parson Wems. 'But I doubt (shaking his head) whether the hearts of many were not barred and bolted against me.'"[7]

Parson Weems was not content knocking at the front door with his preaching. As a writer, he might be said to have tried the side door: as a bookseller, he joined forces with a Catholic publisher to try the back entrance as well. He made Dumfries his headquarters after his marriage to Frances Ewell, daughter of Col. Jesse Ewell of Bel Air. The Weems and their eight children went to live at Bel Air, about 1808 or 1809.
Courtesy of the Weems-Botts Museum

Dr. W. E. S. Flory, a retired professor who taught business subjects at American University and the present owner of Bel Air, believes that another talent Weems displayed was in the business field of marketing. The principles of successful marketing set fourth in 1963 by General Electric, says Dr. Flory, were to perceive, anticipate, and satisfy customers' needs. Weems's letters to his publisher show his methodology fit the prescription. He realized the clientele of different areas would buy different books. Weems believed his generation must ensure the young had high standards of morality and integrity to enable them to maintain the democratic freedom won by the Revolution. To satisfy this need, the parson used another twentieth-century concept: he provided role models in his biographies of Washington, Franklin, and Francis Marion, the Swamp Fox.[8] Courtesy of Dr. W. E. S. Flory

Washington's first biographer, Mason Locke Weems.

The western section of Prince William and its neighbors had been quietly filling with settlers after the exit of the Indians in 1722. A number of third and fourth generation Carter heirs had moved north to claim their portions of the 41,600 acre Bull Run Tract. It would be inaccurate to view the plantations in western Prince William as a sign of spontaneous economic growth however. Fairfax Harrison called them rather "The Barrier of the Manors."

Coming from England before the Industrial Revolution, the early settlers in Virginia hoped to establish themselves and their posterity in power by means of land ownership. Those charged with the responsibility of making land grants appropriated for themselves enormous tracts of land. They expected settlers arriving after all the northern Virginia land was granted to become tenants on the established estates. So long as there was land to be had to the west, however, settlers chose to move in the direction of the great river valleys of the mid-continent, where, by a kind of poetic justice, the richest farmland was and still is. The population of Prince William County in 1790 was almost identical with the population in 1900—just over eleven thousand people. After the Revolution, Virginia became a "feeder state." Blacks were sold to plantation owners farther south, and whites departed seeking opportunity in the west.[4]

While many left Prince William in the early nineteenth century, their lands were often bought by incoming northern farmers, mostly from New York state and New Jersey, many of them members of the Society of Friends, (Quakers). Partly because the Quakers were opposed to slavery, and partly because cotton and tobacco do not grow well here, large farms or plantations using slave labor were not the rule in Prince William by the middle of the nineteenth century. Virginia's black population was 43.4 percent of the total in 1790 and 43.3 percent in 1860. The natural increase in slave families were being sold to

One reason Occoquan drew so few settlers at first is suggested by Davis also. On his way from Colchester, he noted, "...so steep and craggy was the road, that I found it almost inaccessible. On descending the last hill (coming up the Occoquan from the Potomac), I was nearly stunned by the noise of two huge mills, whose roar, without any hyperbolical aggravation, is scarcely inferior to that of the great fall of the Potomac, or the cataract of Niagara." The Ellicott mill, of which Davis was speaking, was among the first to employ automated flour machinery. It was invented by Oliver Evans of Wilmington, Delaware, in 1795.

The larger of the two mills in the picture, taken many years afterward when the road was not quite so inaccessible, is the flour mill built by the Ellicotts which continued operations until it burned in 1924. The thunderous noise Davis wrote of might have been explained by magnification within the high banks of the swift flowing stream, or he might have been listening to three water wheels and six sets of millstones going at the same time. This is what Thomas Ellicott, writing for a London publication in 1796, stated was "planned and built by me on Occoquam."[10]
Courtesy of Hilda Cline Brown Ammerman

The Janney brothers, like the Ellicotts, were members of the Society of Friends. In 1828, they added another mill, a cotton spinning mill of one thousand spindles. Annie McCracken, born in Quebec of Scottish parents, was brought to Occoquan to train the girls who ran the spindles. During her stay in Occoquan, she met and married Magruder Keys, himself a descendent of Scottish immigrants who came to Prince William and obtained a land grant in colonial times. This picture was probably taken after the Civil War, when the Keys and any of their thirteen children still at home were living at "Cedar Hill," the Keys family farm, which is now a part of Prince William Forest Park.[12]
Courtesy of Hilda Cline Brown Ammerman

planters farther south, where additional labor was needed. In 1860, moreover, one of every six blacks counted in the census was free.[5]

As Dumfries declined, the farmers of western Prince William sent their goods to Alexandria by way of the Warrenton Turnpike Road, which branched off from the Little River Turnpike Road at Fairfax Court House. The Warrenton company was chartered in 1807 and had built the road all the way to Orange Court House by 1827.[6]

An even more important factor in the economic life of Prince William in the second half of the nineteenth century was the advent of the Orange and Alexandria Railroad. In 1852 the line reached the little junction at Tudor Hall, where a spur line ran into the Shenandoah Valley through Manasseh's Gap. The iron rails were to bring commerce and invaders to western Prince William, as the river had done for the east.

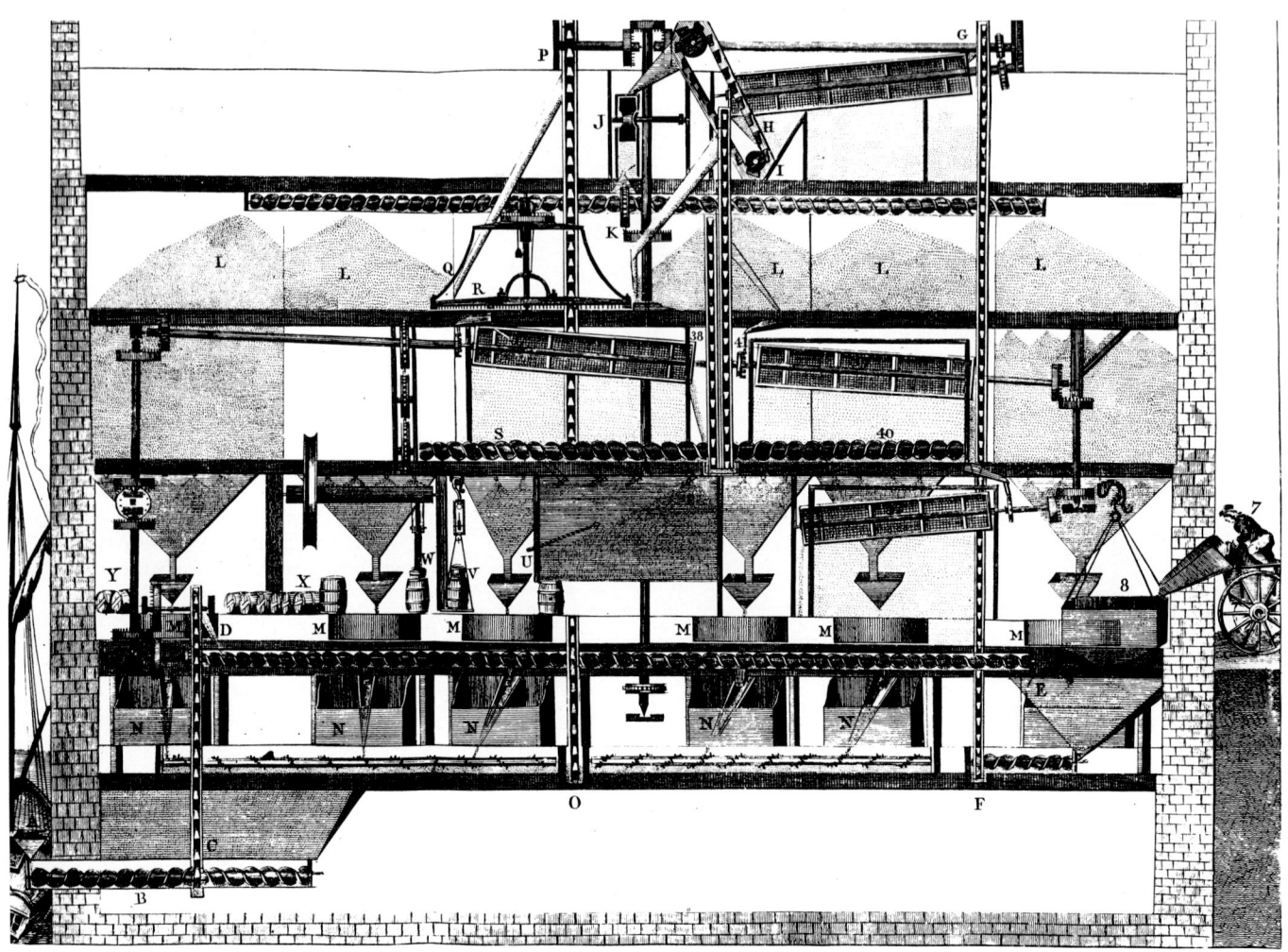

In the introduction to the plan of his new mill, Thomas Ellicott reported his automated process saved two to three pounds of waste per bushel, from spillage, dust, improper grinding, etc. To understand how this was done, start at "Z" on the bottom left of the picture, where a ship has come alongside the mill. A grain sack is emptied into the hopper (A) which shunts it onto the conveyor (B) which takes the grain to the elevator (C). (The elevator is an endless strap filled with small wood or sheet iron buckets which fill and empty themselves.) The conveyor (D) takes grain to the hopper-garner (E). This goes to the main wheat elevator (F), and on to the roof and rolling screen (G above the collar beams) where it falls into the hopper (H) and goes to the short elevator (I). This takes the grain to the fan (J). (Steps A thru J were a kind of cleaning process.) From the fan (J) the grain runs down the slanting tube to a long conveyor (K), running to both ends of the mill, dropping grain along the way into any of the garners (L) over the millstones (M). (The grain is supposed to be fed in turn to different millstones by shifting a board under the cogwheel (K). Each garner holds two thousand bushels of wheat, twelve thousand bushels in all. By this method the feeding is more evenly done than formerly.) As the wheat is ground by the millstones, it falls to the meal conveyors (N), which take it to the meal elevator (O). This raises it to (P) and it runs down to the hopper boy (Q), which spreads and cools it over an area ten to fifteen feet in diameter. Thirty or more barrels of flour at a time can be put into the bolting hoppers (R), on to the conveyors (S) and the hole (T) in the floor and to the packing chest for mixing and packing in the barrels (U). This goes to the weighing device (V) and packing (W) and is then headed and rolled to the door (Y) where it is lowered back to the ship it came from. Wheat which comes overland by wagon is dumped in on the opposite side of the mill (E) which takes it to the elevator (F) and so through the same procedure.[11] *Courtesy of the Library of Congress*

This model of "Cedar Hill" was made for Annie Keys Shumate by her second husband, the Rev. Albert Shumate, a Methodist minister. Mrs. Shumate was very fond of her grandmother, Annie McCracken Keys, for whom the little one-story addition was built after the death of Magruder Keys in 1886.
Courtesy of Hilda Cline Brown Ammerman

Robert Tansill was born on a farm near Occoquan and, after a somewhat stormy career in the U.S. Marines, settled down in Manassas and became one of its first mayors. Tansill was aboard a ship that accompanied Commodore Matthew Galbraith Perry to Japan in 1853. In 1861 he resigned his commission from a ship in the harbor at Montevideo, Uruguay, to join the Confederate forces.[13]
Courtesy of G. E. and Jane MacDonald

It was customary to be buried in little cemeteries on the family farms. Robert Tansill is buried beside his first wife, Frances Weems, on a farm in southern Prince William County. A granddaughter of Parson Weems, she died only a year after their wedding at Bel Air. Tansill's best man was Fanny's cousin, Richard Ewell, who became a well known Civil War general.
Courtesy of G. E. and Jane MacDonald

Also in the Prince William Forest Park area was the farm home shown here, known as "Grinstead," owned by Thomas Nelson, and the ruins of Nelson's mill. The young lady standing on the steps is Virginia Speiden Carper of Manassas, great-granddaughter of Thomas Nelson.[14]
Courtesy of Virginia Speiden Carper

Thomas Nelson's son, Edwin, married his cousin, Bettie Weedon, who also grew up "below the Run." In Prince William parlance, this refers to the land lying south and east of Broad Run. The young Nelsons lived in Brentsville where he became clerk of the county court, and later in Manassas.
Courtesy of Virginia Speiden Carper

Betsy Bates, a free black woman listed in the 1830 census, born between 1795 and 1805, was the ancestress of families living in what was called "Batestown," now a part of Prince William Forest Park. Longtime residents of Dumfries sometimes refer to Mine Road as the Batestown Road, because it led to Batestown as well as to the pyrite mine. Wilmer Porter, the first black man elected to municipal office in Virginia since Reconstruction, is a descendent of Betsy Bates.[15]
Courtesy of Wilmer and Mary Porter

*Mount Atlas, a plantation home in the foothills of the Bull Run Mountains, is thought to have been built about 1795. Like many houses of that day, it was built without an inside kitchen. Slaves carried the meals to the second story dining room along a flagstone walk from a four-room kitchen and slave cabin in the garden.[16]
Courtesy of Pauline Padgett*

*Willis Foley, born in 1780, bought Mount Atlas and its surrounding 897-acre plantation in 1836. In this early photograph, Mr. Foley is wearing the "high cravat" or black silk neckerchief, brocaded waistcoat, and linen shirt, fashions in favor from 1840 into the 1850s.[17]
Courtesy of Pauline Padgett*

*Shown here is Mrs. Willis Foley, born Nancy Randolph Mallory in 1786. The crack in the glass, which is the actual picture, shows this to be a very early form of photography called Ambrotype. Mrs. Foley is wearing a ruched and ruffled cap of fine white cotton and a dress with drop shoulders and pointed bodice over a hoop skirt. Like her husband's attire, these were fashions popular during the 1840s and 1850s. Mrs. Foley died in 1857. Ambrotype was especially popular in the 1850s.[18]
Courtesy of Pauline Padgett*

Antioch Baptist Church, built in 1837 on land given by William Foley, father of Willis Foley, from his Poplar Hall plantation. This stone building with its separate entrances for men and women was torn down in 1901 to make way for a larger frame building.[19]
Courtesy of Pauline Padgett

Not far from Antioch Baptist Church, on the Mountain Road, stands LaGrange. This plantation home, built in 1790, is still used as a private residence.
Courtesy of Marianna Durst

Buckland Tavern on the old Warrenton-Alexandria Turnpike Road came very close to falling down before Grace Bear bought and restored it in the early 1940s. In the heyday of the turnpike road, from 1824 until the Civil War, Buckland Tavern was a place where wagon drivers, the teamsters of a century ago, stopped to water their animals and have a meal. It is also reputed to have been one of the places where the Marquis de Lafayette was honored at dinner during the French hero's triumphal tour in 1825. The route of the turnpike from Warrenton to Fairfax Court House in this century became a part of one of the first "interstates" built by the federal government. This patchwork of improved old roads is still called the Robert E. Lee Highway. In these 1975 photos, prospective buyers are attending an auction at which the tavern was resold.[20]
Courtesy of Mrs. Alma Bridge

Only the filled-in outlines of the arches remind the viewer that St. Paul's Episcopal Church, Haymarket, was built in 1803 as a courthouse. It served as the seat of the district court for the counties of Fauquier, Loudoun, Fairfax, and Prince William from 1803 until 1807. Despite Haymarket's favorable location at a crossroads at the foot of the mountains where the Carolina Road met the road from the coast leading to the Shenandoah Valley, the village languished once the court was moved away. The building became first a school, then a church, a hospital during the Civil War, and, after that, a church once more. Courtesy of Marianna Durst

*Another Piedmont plantation house was Hagley, which stood at the intersection of Waterfall Road and Mount Atlas Lane. The architecture and the massive chimneys suggest it was built in the eighteenth century. Notice the children sitting upon what appears to be a mounting platform for carriages and horseback riders.
Courtesy of Pauline Padgett*

*Pictured at Hagley are: front row, left to right, Annie Foley Smith, Fanny Beale. Back row, Florence Burroughs Smith, Ann Matilda Smith Pickett holding Katherine Ann Pickett.
Courtesy of Pauline Padgett*

*Not far from Hagley and Mount Atlas, on the road across the Blue Ridge to the Shenandoah Valley, stands Chapman's Mill, seen in the background of this nineteenth-century photograph. The first mill was built by Jonathan Chapman about 1760 near a spot where Broad Run makes an eighty-seven-foot drop in a distance of thirteen-hundred feet. The resultant water power was used for two mills: one ground corn and cattle feed; the other, flour. The picture was taken after 1854 when the Manassas Gap Railroad was completed directly behind the mill (in the right of the picture). Autos on Interstate 66 today travel very close to the road used by the horse-drawn buggy in the middle distance.[21]
Courtesy of Manassas National Battlefield Park*

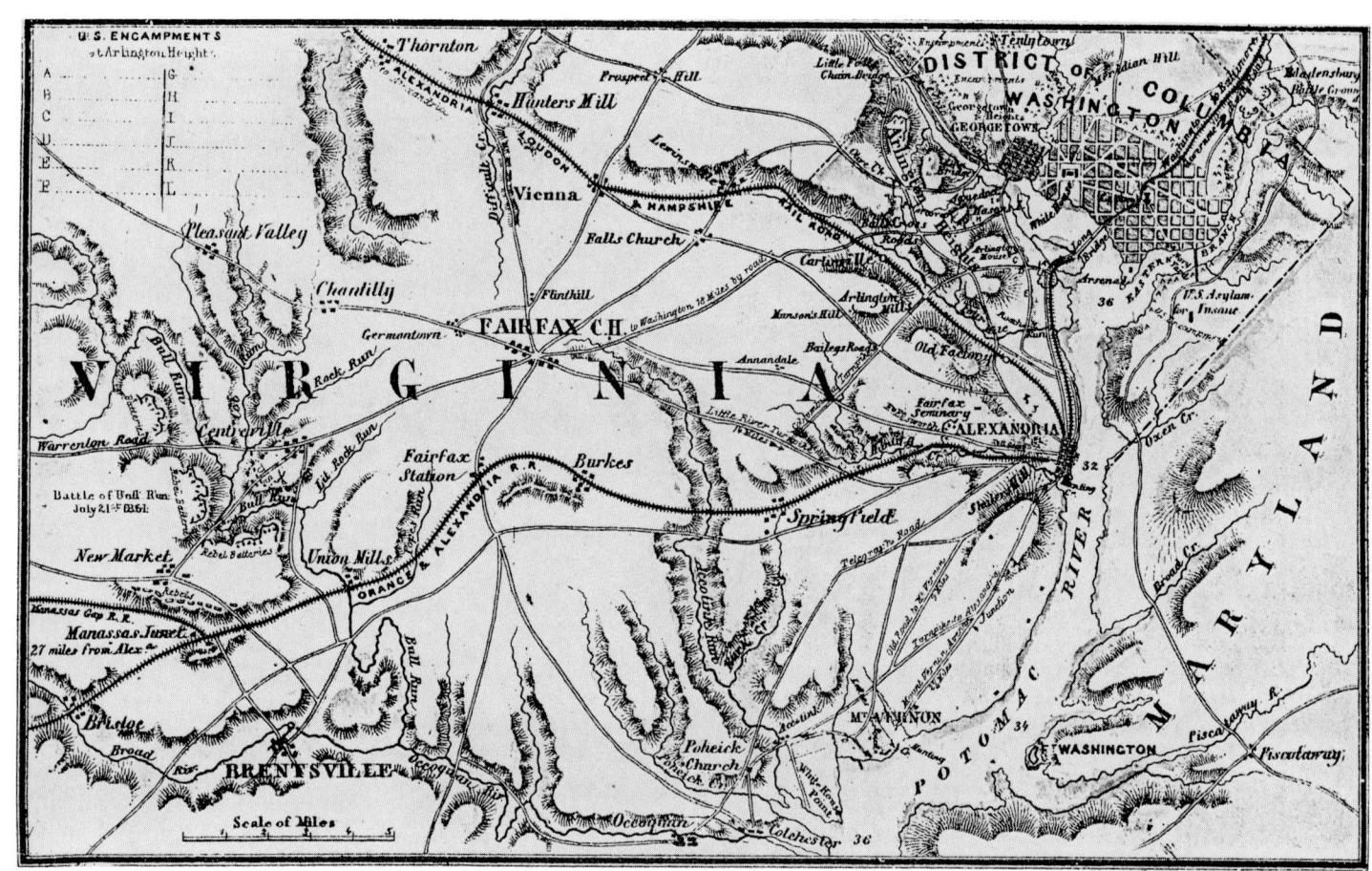

One of the things this 1861 map explains is the use of the term "Washington City" in contemporary references to the national capital. Notice how much of the District of Columbia was still rural during the Civil War. Note also the contrasting size of Brentsville and Manassas Junction. Courtesy of the Virginia Historical Society

CHAPTER 4
ALONG THE RIVER
AND THE RAILROAD

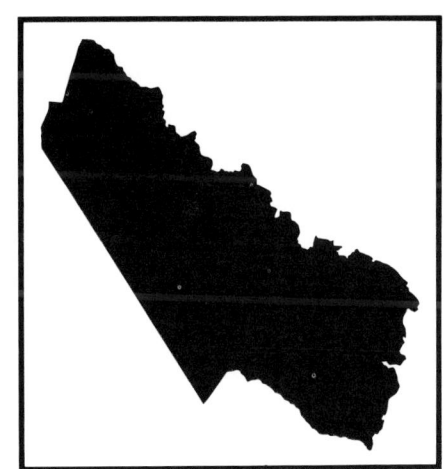

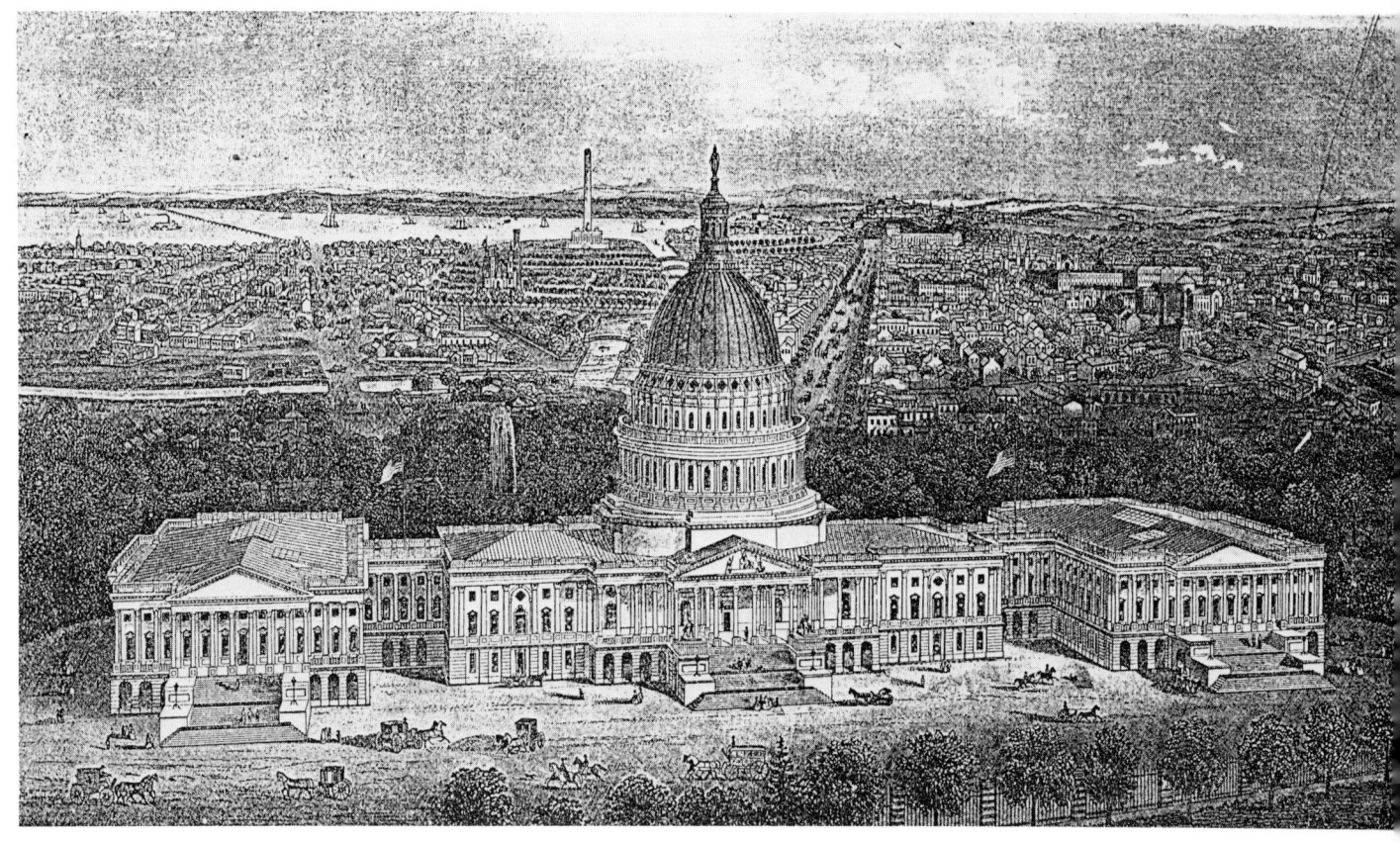

Shortly after May 23, 1861, when Virginia officially joined the Confederacy, the *dramatis personae* of the war began assembling in Prince William County and other sections of Northern Virginia. General P. G. T. Beauregard, newly appointed commander of the Army of Northern Virginia, arrived at Manassas Junction to take command of the troops assembling.[1] In the first year and a half of the conflict, two major battles swirled, like tornadoes, around the little railroad junction. Yet Confederate forces, the nominal victors in both battles, chose to withdraw from Prince William County to more defensible positions near Richmond in early 1862. George Carr Round, writing after the conflict, claimed the Battles of First and Second Manassas or called by Union historians the First and Second Battles of Bull Run, were the only time on record where two great armies fought twice over the same ground with the lines of battle exactly reversed.[2]

One noteworthy occurrence after the first Battle of Manassas (or Bull Run) was the construction of a spur-line to carry supplies to the Southern troops quartered at Centreville in neighboring Fairfax County during the winter of 1861 through February 1862. It is believed to be the first rail-line in history to be built solely for military purposes. As the Confederate army retreated to more defensible positions to the south, the supply-line railroad was torn up so the rails could be used elsewhere. Its existence was all but forgotten.

The Potomac River blockade, also almost consigned to oblivion, occurred during the first year of the war. The blockade was effected by batteries of mostly naval guns, captured at the Portsmouth Naval Yard near Norfolk and mounted on bluffs overlooking the Potomac in Prince William County. These guns successfully kept almost all river traffic from proceeding up the Potomac to Washington, D.C. From October 1861 until the army withdrew in March 1862, supplies for the national capital came primarily from the north via the single track of the Baltimore and Ohio Railroad.

From March 1862, when General Johnston's army withdrew, there were Federal troops in Prince William County guarding the supply-lines, except for a brief period after the Battle of Second Manassas and Bristoe Station in 1863. More troops were tied up protecting supply-lines than would have been used had it not been for the guerilla activities of Mosby's Rangers.

The war brought destruction and economic ruin to Prince William. It was many years before the farms and homes in the battle area returned to normal. Many farms that were burned or destroyed were rebuilt, but others were not. Numerous returning soldiers went west to make a new start. A good deal of the rebuilding was done by new residents from the north and other parts of the south, who moved in after the war.

The Chinn House, circa 1880 on the left, and the Matthews house, circa 1900, below, are two of the homes that the armies may have seen as they marched through Prince William and fought over its fords and fields.
Courtesy of the Manassas National Battlefield Park

Sudley Ford across Catharpin Run, also known as Little Bull Run, was used as a troop crossing at the beginning of the Battle of First Manassas (or Bull Run). The Methodist Church on the knoll in the background canceled services that day. These two photographs were taken by G. N. Barnard circa 1862.
Courtesy of the Manassas National Battlefield Park

This is Sudley Ford from the opposite side, taking in the area supposed to have mineral properties. After the Civil War, when such bathing places were popular, a hotel was built by the ford in an effort to create a spa.
Courtesy of the Manassas National Battlefield Park

"Portici", the house with the large brick chimneys, was one of the homes of the Carter heirs. The owner, Alfred Ball, in 1851, sold Avon Farm to Abraham Van Pelt, a newcomer from New Jersey.
Courtesy of the Manassas National Battlefield Park

The house shown may be the clapboarded log house originally on the property, one of the oldest buildings in Prince William, built circa 1850. The photograph was taken circa 1900, and the house burned in 1936.
Courtesy of the Manassas National Battlefield Park

In 1855 Ball sold twenty-six acres and the other house shown to James Robinson, a free black man. This photograph taken circa 1864, pictured the rear side of Robinson's home.
Courtesy of the Manassas National Battlefield Park

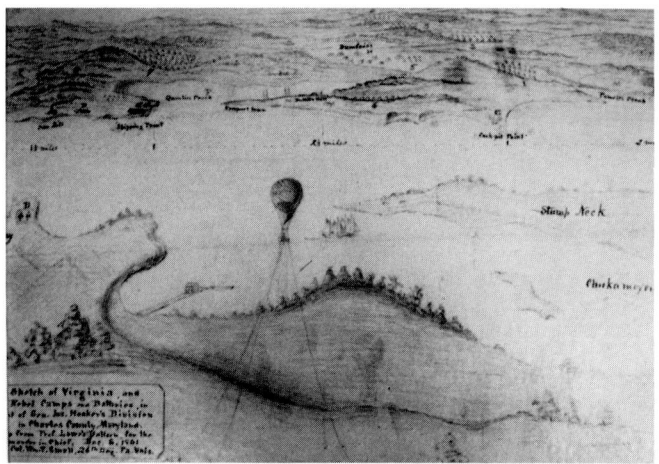

The sketch made from Prof. Thaddeus Lowe's famous balloon on the Maryland side does not include the battery of guns on Freestone Point as shown on Karen White's 1986 map.
Courtesy of the National Archives

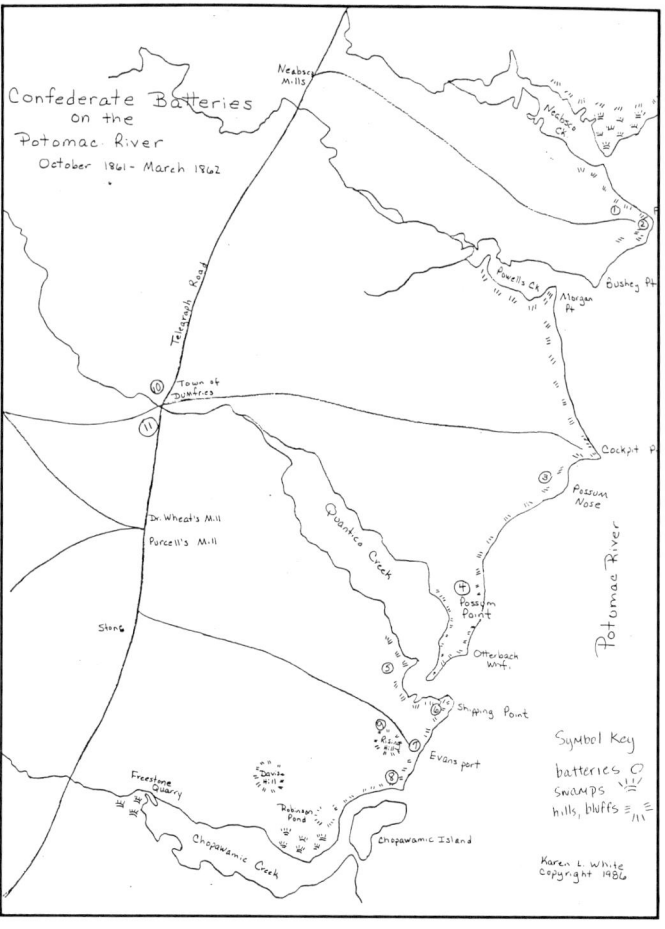

Courtesy of Karen L. White

Confederates from this log fort at the junction, called Camp Pickens, left with the rest of the Southern forces in March 1862, burning what they could not take.
Courtesy of the Manassas National Battlefield Park

Artist Alfred R. Waud made this pictorial representation of the occasion, which appeared in Harper's Weekly, *March 29, 1862.*
Courtesy of the Library of Congress

An unknown photographer recorded the ruined turntable after the 1862 withdrawal. Both sides became very adept at rebuilding the railroads, so by 1864, the only suggestion of wartime is the desolation in the background.
Courtesy of the Manassas National Battlefield Park

The Army of the Potomac crossed Kettle Run, pictured here by Edwin Forbes on the morning of the Battle of Bristoe Station, October 14, 1863. As they passed through Prince William they would have seen scenes such as those described by Robert E. Lee, Jr., in a letter to his mother that same month. "All that country the other side of Warrenton—along the R.R. and east of it is a perfect desert, not a dwelling but that is torn all to pieces, not a piece of fencing or any signs of civilization except one or two families principally free negroes."[1]
Courtesy of the Library of Congress

Chapman's Mill in Thoroughfare Gap was used by the Confederate Army as a meat packing plant in the early stages of the war. When they withdrew they burned the mill and its contents. The shell seen in this photo was rebuilt and became the property of William Beverly in 1870. It continued as a regional merchant's mill, grinding corn and plaster until after World War II.[2]
Courtesy of the Manassas National Battlefield Park

Occoquan was the scene of fighting on several occasions. Here, in January 1862, Union troops attacked Wade Hampton's division, protecting the battery of guns on Freestone Point. It was after a similar raid by General J. E. B. Stuart's cavalry on Union forces holding the town the following December that John S. Mosby was left behind to begin his guerrilla operations. Mosby was very astute in pinpointing the weak spots in Union lines and in harassing civilians such as the sutlers shown here. Courtesy of the Library of Congress

HARPER'S WEEKLY.
A JOURNAL OF CIVILIZATION.

Vol. VII.—No. 349.] NEW YORK, SATURDAY, SEPTEMBER 5, 1863. [SINGLE COPIES SIX CENTS. $2.50 PER YEAR IN ADVANCE.

MOSEBY'S GUERRILLAS DESTROYING SUTLERS' TRAIN.—[SEE PAGE 567.]

No one would have predicted that one of the best liked and most influential men in Manassas after the war would be an ex-Yankee, a former U.S. Army Signal Corps officer from New England, but it was so. This picture of George Carr Round was taken about 1861 shortly after he left Connecticut Wesleyan College at the end of his junior year to enlist in the Union Army. After the war, he returned to finish his degree, and graduated with a Phi Beta Kappa key. He then added a law degree from Columbia University in New York to his credentials before heading south.

The young man had originally intended going to North Carolina, where his first cousins lived. It was in Raleigh he had spent the final days of the war, in charge of a signal station on the dome of the capitol. Very early in the morning of what was to be the last day of the war came the word that the army had been waiting to hear: General Johnston had agreed to follow General Lee's lead and lay down his arms.

Lieutenant Round asked and received permission to use his signal rockets to spell out the news to the men camped on the lands around the city. He realized at least one outpost of the Army of the Tennessee understood the message: they sent up such a shout, Round later wrote, as the shepherds might have done, when they read in the skies over Bethlehem that same message he was transmitting, "Peace on earth, good will toward men." It was a moment the young officer spoke of the rest of his life.[1]

However, when Round began his life work, in the words of a popular Civil War song, helping to "put the lost stars in the flag once again," he got off the train in Virginia instead of North Carolina. Courtesy of the Manassas City Museum

CHAPTER 5

GATEWAY TO A NEW CENTURY

This brick home called Liberia belonged to the Weirs, a family of Carter heirs, who owned a great deal of land where the central business district of Manassas is now. As one of the largest and most desirable homes in the vicinity, Liberia was used as headquarters by Northern and Southern commanders alike.
Courtesy of the Manassas City Museum

One of the most notable differences in Prince William County after the War Between the States was the rise to prominence of the town that grew at the former railroad junction of Manassas in the west central part of the county. That hamlet mushroomed rapidly after 1865, due in part to the efforts of an energetic Northern immigrant, George Carr Round.

It was the junction with the line to the Shenandoah Valley which kept Manassas from remaining Tudor Hall—just another little waystop on the Orange and Alexandria. The state legislature gave Manassas its town charter in 1873. The newly fledged town then petitioned to supercede Brentsville as the county seat, but was voted down. The reason for the petition, of course, was that Manassas was easily accessible by rail and Brentsville was not. Those with a commercial stake in the Brentsville location blocked a change in 1872 and again in 1888, but the third petition and referendum in 1892 was successful. Manassas became the county seat. The mills and plantations were slowly rebuilt.

The railway did not play such a significant part in the eastern half of the county. Although the final link between Richmond and Washington was built after the war, land use of the former river plantations took on a different aspect there.

Education was to play a much more important part than before. Several praiseworthy efforts to establish colleges were made, but the greatest need was at the elementary and secondary levels. Here again George Carr Round was active. He considered education of special importance and was active in helping the establishment of the Manassas Academy, which became a public high school. He also encouraged and supported the work of the daughter of two former slaves, Jennie Dean, founder of the Manassas Vocational Industrial School for Colored Youth, which gave her fellow blacks an opportunity to get an education.

Both Abraham Lincoln and Jefferson Davis may have stood before this living room mantle at Liberia. It is reputed to be the only home visited by both commanders in chief.
Courtesy of the Library of Congress

*Once the decision to move the county seat from Brentsville to Manassas had been made in 1892, one of the first to relocate was the clerk of the circuit court, Edwin Nelson. He and his wife are shown here, far left, with their family at their new home on Battle Street. To the immediate right of Mr. and Mrs. Nelson are their daughter Elizabeth and her husband, Austin Weedon, who later became mayor of neighboring Warrenton in Fauquier County. The Weedons' two children, Austin and Elizabeth, are also in the picture. Next to the Weedons on the back row are the Nelsons' other daughter, Effie, and her husband, architect Albert Speiden. The Nelsons' son, John Horatio, an attorney, is holding the family dog, while his brother James Edwin, an accountant, holds a picture representing the third brother, Paul, who was attending Virginia Military Institute. After Paul's graduation, he went to work in West Virginia, where he met and married Mary Robson. They named the summer home they built in Manassas Robnel. Although the house is gone, the name is perpetuated in the subdivision that stands on the land where it was located.
Courtesy of Virginia Speiden Carper*

*Edwin Nelson liked to relax in his sunny backyard and enjoy granddaughter Virginia Speiden, who lived next door. Nelson bought this home because it was within easy walking distance of the courthouse. Before he owned the house, it had belonged to Mr. and Mrs. F. W. Hynson and previously to Mayor and Mrs. Robert Tansill.
Courtesy of Virginia Speiden Carper*

*After Mr. and Mrs. Edwin Nelson died in 1911, their home was sold. One hot summer day in 1914, the house caught fire and burned. Since there was no city water at that time, the Speiden home next door was only saved by the cistern on its roof. The firemen used the water in the cistern to supply their hoses. As the spray was played over the flames on the roof, it fell back into the cistern and was recycled.
  Fire was a serious scourge at that time. In December 1905, a fire burned a block and a half of downtown Manassas. The town of Occoquan, on the bank of a river, was almost destroyed by fire in August, 1916.[2]
Courtesy of Virginia Speiden Carper*

Architect Albert Speiden could claim to be a Virginian even before he married Effie Nelson and moved to Manassas, since he was born at his family's summer home on Seminary Hill outside Alexandria. Although Speiden commuted by train to his office in Washington, he designed many buildings, both public and residential, in Manassas.
Courtesy of Virginia Speiden Carper

According to his daughter, Albert Speiden liked best to design churches. Every church in Manassas and some outside the city had his work in them, whether original design or modification. When the Sudley Methodist Church in Catharpin was struck by lightning and burned in 1918, the congregation ordered new plans from Speiden and it was rebuilt. Manassas Baptist Church as shown here was where Mr. and Mrs. Speiden were married. However, it was not at that time a recipient of his work.[3]
Courtesy of Virginia Speiden Carper

Not every architect's daughter is as lucky as Virginia Speiden was when her father gave her this dollhouse. It was meant to be authentic as well as attractive and a reminder of her girlhood. Because Manassas had no electric lights or city power before 1914, the dollhouse has oil lamps and candles. Neither was there city water nor indoor plumbing, so the dolls had a chamber pot, and a miniature outhouse (not shown).
Courtesy of the author

Each room is filled with replicas of what would have been there in the early twentieth century. (Note the Bissel carpet sweeper standing in the corner, the treadle sewing machine, and the brass bedstead.)
Courtesy of the author

Among the kitchen equipment of the World War I era are the woodburning stove, the iron that would have been heated on it, and the washtub and scrub board. Virginia liked to pretend the dolls had gone for a walk and she herself lived in the house.
Courtesy of the author

Among ther stately Victorian homes at turn of the century Manassas, Annaburg Manor stood out as the showplace. It was the summer home of Mr. and Mrs. Robert Portner. Portner had come over from Germany and made his fortune operating a brewery in Alexandria. Annaburg was named for Mrs. Portner, who was also German. On the grounds at Annaburg Portner replicated a ruined tower like one in his homeland. The Portners were very civic minded and their home was the scene of much entertaining. The grounds were used for special events. In the late nineteenth century, Mr. Portner, who was also inventive, installed what may have been the first air conditioning in the United States in his home. Today, Annaburg is a nursing home.
Courtesy of the Manassas City Museum

About the time of World War I, George Round (front row, second from left) led a delegation of his fellow citizens, dressed in their best, to Washington. Whatever their errand may have been, no one today remembers. It does not appear to have been an angry protest, judging from the expressions on their faces, standing on the steps near the White House to have their picture taken.
Courtesy of Virginia Speiden Carper

It is no wonder Manassas residents felt comfortable visiting the White House. They could be returning the call the President paid them to celebrate the fiftieth anniversary of the First Battle of Bull Run (or Manassas). George Carr Round orchestrated a memorial reunion of the veterans from the North and South held in front of the Prince William County Court House in Manassas. Far from re-enacting the ordeal, one thousand of the survivors from both armies walked across the field and shook hands as a gesture of friendship. The pretty girls in cheesecloth dresses seated at the rear of the platform represented the states. Ruth Round, George Round's daughter, took the part of Rhode Island, his mother's home. Center stage in this photo of the Peace Jubilee on July 21, 1911, were President William Howard Taft and Governor William Hodges Mann of Virginia.
Courtesy of the Manassas City Museum

POSTCARDS

Photographers of the twentieth century discovered a wonderful way to market their wares—pictures of local landmarks on cards that travelers might use to show their progress to the folks back home. W. N. Wenrich, a local jeweler who was also a photographer, sold postcards through Dowell's Pharmacy in Manassas. Others were made and marketed in Manassas by photographers in Washington, D.C., and Arneville, North Carolina.
Courtesy of the author

In the 1930s, Manasses was listed in a national newspaper column as the town in the United States with the most churches per capita. This is one of them, the Presbyterian Church. The church figured as background in "My Son John," a controversial Hollywood production, released in the spring of 1952. Sans the steeple, the church has since become a restaurant, "La Chapelle."
Courtesy of the author

The postcard of Portner's Prince William Hotel can be dated earlier, partly because the elegant establishment, built in 1904, burned in 1910, and certainly because a traveler posted it on September 13, 1906, in a receptacle at the train station. Without ever going through the regular Manassas post office, such epistles were put on the train and processed in transit by the clerk of the mail car, proceeding along the route of the old Manassas Gap line in the "Washington and Harrisonburg Railroad Post Office." Not only did the post office not require a zip code in those simpler days, no street address was necessary for some areas. The address on this card is simply "Miss Fleming, Richmond, Indiana."
Courtesy of the author

As benefitted a town that was both a rail junction and a county seat, hotels might expect good trade. Shown here are two early twentieth-century establishments featured on postcards. The architecture of the Stonewall Jackson indicates its 1912 beginning, but the restaurant sign at the side suggests the photo may have been taken in the 1930s.
Courtesy of the author

54

This comfortable turn of the century house, the domicile of the Baldwin family, overlooked the Southern Railway depot across from the business section of Manassas. It was to become Baldwin Hall, the nucleus of an ambitious scheme to locate a small college in Northern Virginia. Courtesy of the Manassas City Museum

Eastern College was one of two schools in Manassas with out-of-town students. It was moved from Front Royal in 1909. In 1914, when a female student named Kathryn sent this card to a Miss Ruth Todd in Christiana, Lancaster County, Pennsylvania, the college may have been at its zenith. Students were enrolled from as many as twenty-two states and two foreign countries. East and Voorhees Hall contained both dormitories and classrooms, which must have made student life easier in bad weather. World War I created a financial crisis for the little school. To make up for the anticipated loss of male students in 1917, Eastern obtained a government contract to train military personnel. Expensive alterations were called for by the contract, but had barely been finished when the war ended. The resultant financial strain closed the college after the school year of 1919 through 1920. A faculty member, Mr. B. Templeton Hodge, taught law and Greek.

There was a brief unsuccessful trial as a music conservatory for young ladies, then an eleven-year period (1924 through 1935) when the buildings housed the Swavely School for Boys. This was a preparatory school for West Point and Annapolis. Until 1966, the college buildings stood on the little knoll overlooking the railroad depot. After their demolition, the spot became a park and was earmarked as the site of the City Museum in 1988. Portrait courtesy of the Manassas City Museum collection, postcard courtesy of the author

Students were prepared for vocational occupations at the Manassas Industrial School for Colored Youth, also near the railroad tracks on the outskirts of the little town. The school was founded by Jennie Dean, a daughter of former slaves from the Catharpin area. Dean, who had gone to work in the city, realized that young people needed training and education if they were to succeed. Through her own efforts she succeeded in raising funds to build and staff this school. In 1938 the school became part of the public school system. It later became a regional high school for black students from Prince William, Fairfax, Fauquier, and Rappahannock counties. Courtesy of the author

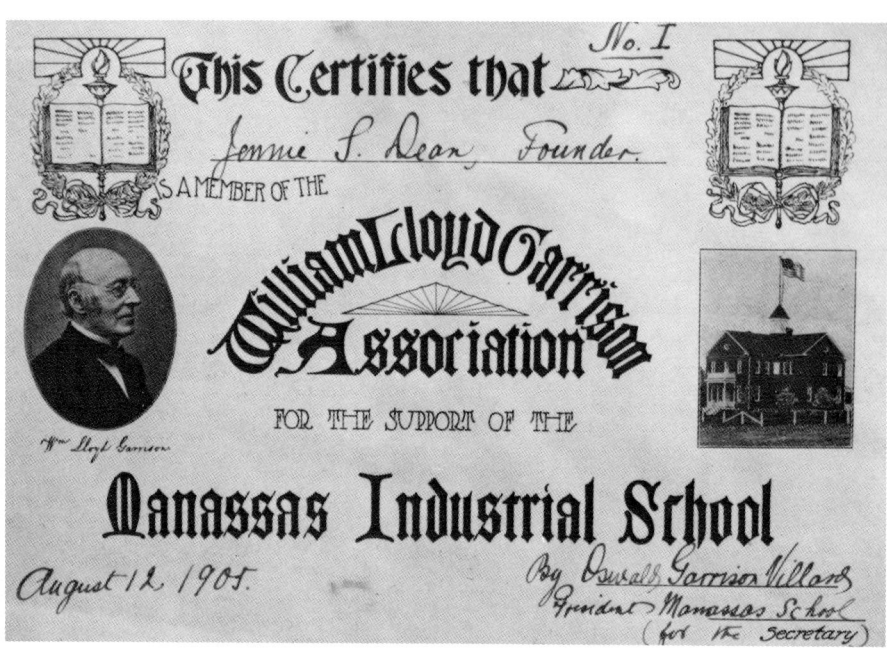

One extant piece of evidence from Jennie Dean's fundraising tours is this certificate in the possession of her niece, Annie Bailey Rose of Alexandria. Rose grew up in Occoquan and remembers spending pleasant summers with her Aunt Jennie. When she was old enough, Annie Bailey attended the Manassas Industrial School. She remembers the students had summer jobs in Northern homes to help pay for their schooling and to gain experience, much as high school and college students today are given credit for on-the-job training.
Courtesy of Annie Bailey Rose

Two other vocational training schools started in Prince William County were St. Joseph's and St. Anne's near Bristow. Both were located on the old plantation of Lintonsford. The last Linton heir, Sarah Linton, born in 1822, spent most of her life as Sister Baptista, a Benedictine nun. She bequeathed the plantation to the Order of St. Benedict. Father Julius Pohle arrived from Belmont Abbey, North Carolina, in 1893 to start St. Joseph's School for Boys. The following year he assisted five Sisters from Richmond who came to start the girls' school. The sisters first started St. Edith's, a private boarding school for girls, shown in this photograph from the collection of the Sisters of the Order of St. Benedict. Profits from St. Edith's as well as donations from church patrons enabled the Benedictine sisters to open St. Anne's, an orphanage and occupational training school for girls, also at Lintonsford, in 1897. St. Anne's was later enlarged and became the guest house as well, shown in the bottom photograph from the Manassas City Museum collection. St. Edith's pictured here was a three-story front added to the first frame building in 1908. All the school facilities were in one building, including the Sisters' dormitory.
Courtesy of the Sisters of the Order of St. Benedict

St. Edith's was closed in 1922, and a military school for boys, ages six to fifteen opened in its place. This new home for the school was built in 1948. Linton Hall Military Academy was replaced in 1988 by a co-educational day school, better suited to the needs of the community, according to a survey taken recently.[6]
Courtesy of the Sisters of the Order of St. Benedict

For a few short years it looked as though education might keep the Summit House in Brentsville solvent after the county seat was moved to Manassas. Although its primary function supposedly was as a summer resort, the hotel must have depended to some extent on patronage from travelers with business at the county seat. When this was withdrawn, the building was rented as a dormitory to the Normal School run by the Baptist Brethren. Classes were held in the old courthouse.
Courtesy of Robert Beahm

This is the 1899 student body and, presumably, the faculty and their families. The Brentsville Academy or Prince William Normal School lasted from 1897 to 1906 or 1907. The designation "Normal School" was common in the United States at that time, a derivative of the French Ecole Normal, meaning a training school for teachers.[7]
Courtesy of Robert Beahm

*In 1909 the Brethren-run school was moved to Nokesville to this building, which, like East and Voorhees halls at Eastern College, contained both sleeping quarters and classrooms. It was renamed Hebron Seminary and functioned as a high school rather than a teachers' college. The building stood at the location of the present-day Church of the Brethren.
Courtesy of Marie Caton*

*The fact that Nokesville was on the railroad may have had some bearing on the move, as well as the fact it put the school in the midst of its sponsoring community. At the turn of the century, high schools were a rarity. Many students had to go to another town to attend. If they lived on the railroad, they might be able to go back and forth rather than live with relatives while they went to a school beyond commuting distance. This situation was true even as late as the 1930s, when this picture was taken.
Courtesy of Marie Caton*

*The president of Hebron Seminary for many years was M. G. Early, shown here with his family about 1891. Left to right: Ola Early Herring, Ella Early Flory, Mr. Early, Daisy Early Crumpacker, Mattie Early nee Martha Miller, Alverta Early Beahm, and Mary Early Davis. Not born in time to be in the picture was Leila Early.
Courtesy of Robert Beahm*

In 1883 Michael G. Early came across the Blue Ridge looking for land to buy, and chose to settle in Nokesville. Early did not share the view of the Ewell family who nicknamed their Nokesville home "Stony Lonesome."[8] In fact he urged his fellow church members back in Rockingham County to come with him where good land was available cheap. This is the two-hundred-acre farm Early bought and named East View. The small rear section of the farmhouse, just visible at the left of the picture, was the house on the property when the Earlys arrived. They added the front section.
Courtesy of Robert Beahm

In 1907 Early had a retirement sale. The poster gives some idea of what a prosperous farmer might own after twenty or thirty years.
Courtesy of Robert Beahm

NEAR NOKESVILLE

Tuesday, Dec. 10, 1907
Commencing at 10 O'Clock, A. M.

I will sell at public auction, on my farm, "East View," one-half mile West of Nokesville, Va., on the above named date, the following:

Nine head of horses (3 of them good brood mares), 2 geldings, 5 and 7 years old, 2 two-year-olds (broken to drive, one of them by Sun Up), and two last spring colts---all of them good ones; 3 young cows, 16 head of young cattle, 3 sows, 19 pigs, small bunch of Southdown sheep.

Wheat binder, corn binder, mower, hayrake, cornplanter, drill, 3 turning plows, sub-soil plow, 2 springtooth harrows, 2 spiketooth harrows, 2 cultivators, double and single shovel plows, forks, shovels, log chains, &c., two-horse wagon, set of low wheels, surrey, 2 buggies, cart, 2 buggy poles, horse power and wood saw, roller, wheat fan, 2 sets wagon harness, double and single buggy harness, saddles, bridles, halters, &c.

Cook and heating stoves, sewing machine, walnut secretary, walnut china press, bureau, bedsteads, chairs, potatoes, &c., &c. Come, rain or shine.

TERMS:---All sums of $10.00 and under, cash; over $10.00 a credit of nine months will be given, the purchaser executing interest bearing negotiable note with approved security, payable at The National Bank Manassas, Va.

S. H. FLORY, Auctioneer.   M. G. EARLY.
PLEASE POST.

The George W. Beahm farm shown here was another of the farms bought by the transplanted congregation of Dunkards or Baptist Brethren. The cattle are typical of the area known in the 1920s as "The Washington Milkshed." Farmers put their milk on the train daily to be sold in Washington.
Courtesy of Robert Beahm

This is how Nokesville looked in 1912 to a human cameraman standing on the first, last, and only oil derrick ever to be built there. The larger white building in the far left rear is Hebron Seminary, which opened three years before. The small house in the right foreground is at the end of the Main Street, now the site of a bank. At one time there were four general stores in Nokesville, supported by the trade of farmers who brought their produce to be shipped on the railroad.
Courtesy of Robert Beahm

This oil derrick was drilled in 1909 on the lands of J. A. Hooker. It proved to be a dry hole.
Courtesy of Robert Beahm

Hebron Seminary operated as a private boarding school from 1909 until 1924. The prospectus emphasized the Christian orientation of the faculty and that students learned moral and spiritual values as well as academic.
Courtesy of Robert Beahm

Starlings

The sun had risen, stillness gripped the day
When from the brindled west I saw appear
An endless column, snake-like, hazy, gray;
And hordes of screaming starlings drifted near.
The leading birds flew low for they had found
An autumn-tinted field of shattered seed
That lay among the clods upon the ground,
Well camouflaged by grass and frosted weed.
They settled down by acres—still they came!
The harshness of their chatter grew tenfold.
The border of the field was now a frame,
The birds a picture, big and black and bold;
A sudden awesome stillness—nothing stirred—
Then blackness lifted skyward as one bird!

—Robert Beahm

Summer Storm

The noontide brilliance of that summer day
Was faded out as low-hung clouds drew near,
They rolled and tossed in somber hues of gray
And caused blue sky to slowly disappear.
Erratic winds increased their staggered pace,
Sure harbinger of fast approaching storms,
While playful lightning streaks began to trace
A jagged diagram of eerie forms.
Long peals of rumbling thunder then I heard!
All sounds of sullen fury were increased!
The angry, moisture-laden clouds, now blurred,
Their pent-up overflow of rain released.
Then everything within my sight was drenched—
The urgent thirst of Mother Earth was quenched.

—Robert Beahm

Pew Ponderings

Prayer coverings three
Sit in front of me—
Ella, Stella, Mary too,
All dressed up in brown and blue,
Ella dozes, nods her head,
She should be at home in bed.
Stella too her head does shake,
But Mary stays quite wide awake.
Other folk around me nod
Here within the House of God;
Since God made this our day of rest
Perhaps in church we do it best!

—Robert Beahm

The guiding light and director of both the Prince William Normal School at Brentsville and the Hebron Seminary was Prof. Isaac Newton Harvey Beahm. At the time of the picture he had left Nokesville and was president of Elizabethtown College and a professional speaker. Organizations which booked Professor Beahm through The Lyceum Bureau could choose to hear his views on: Woman, The Spirit, The Mastery, The Stars and Stripes, The Leading Ideas of Education, and several others.
Courtesy of Robert Beahm

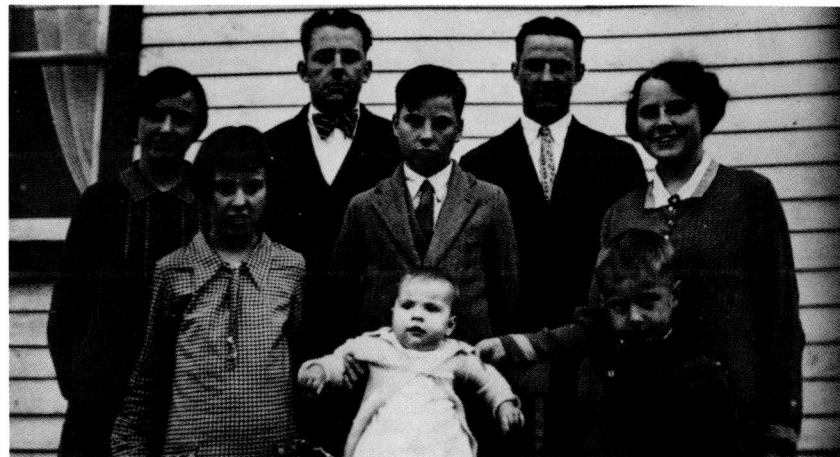

Among Professor Beahm's relatives in Nokesville were the children of his brother George, shown here in 1928. Back row from the left: Cora, Early, and Ralph; in front of them, Ella, Charles, and Hazel Beahm Bucher. In front, held up by her sisters, baby Rosa Lee Beahm Rankin, and Robert. Like his uncle, Robert had a way of weaving thoughts with words. His job as a rural mailman gave his powers of observation and creativity room to work. The poems above may preserve a little of rural Nokesville in the days to come, when the boarded-up dairy farms along Route 28 south of Manassas are full of houses instead of cows.
Courtesy of Robert Beahm

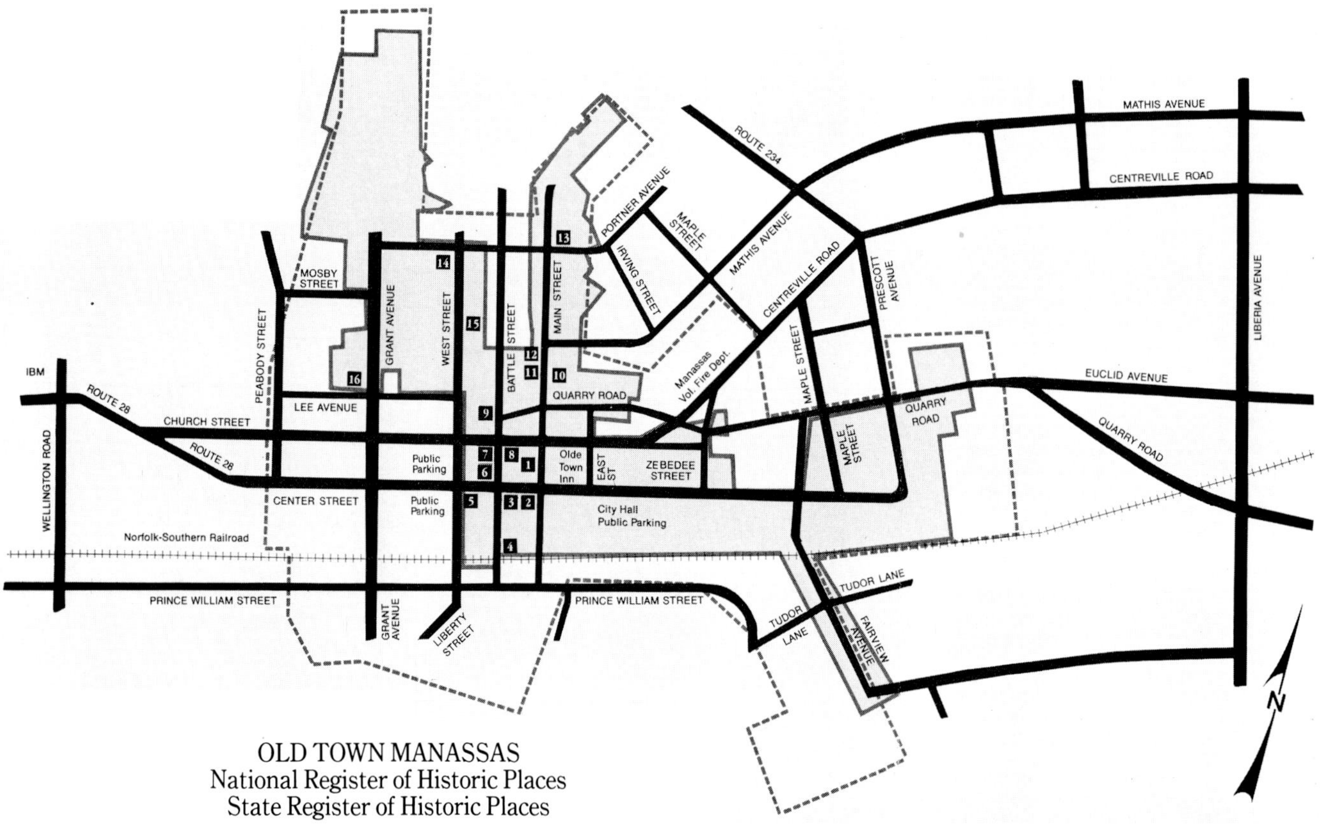

OLD TOWN MANASSAS
National Register of Historic Places
State Register of Historic Places

Map and historical information courtesy of
Historic Manassas and the Manassas City Museum

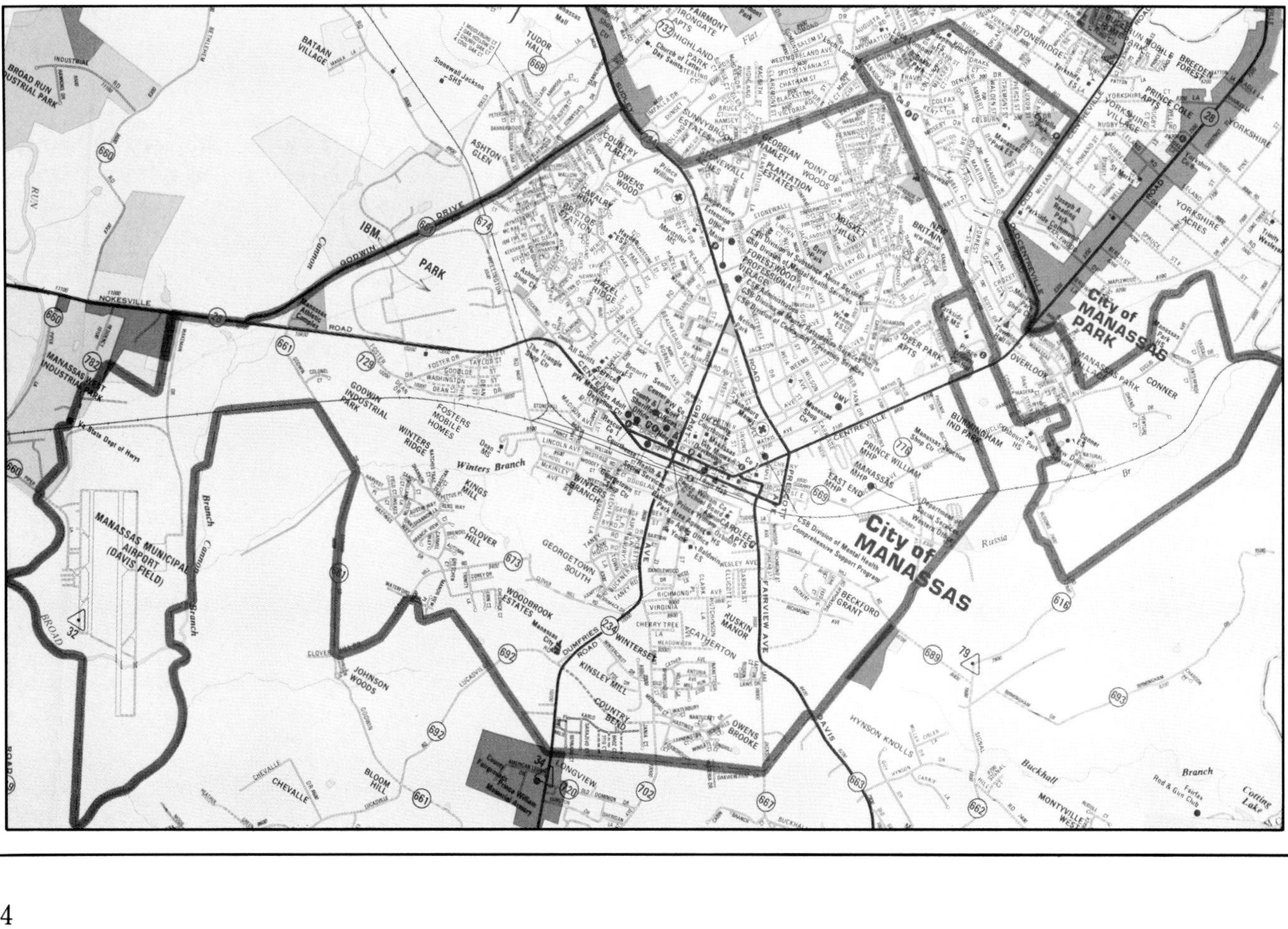

1. **OLD NATIONAL BANK OF MANASSAS**
   9406 Main Street
   The structure has many characteristics of the Victorian Romanesque style, popular at the time of its construction in 1896. Home to the Manassas City Museum since 1973, this two-story building is constructed of brick and red sandstone quarried in Manassas. Note the decorative brickwork, also known as "mousetoothing" in the gable, and the "fishscale" shaped slate on the roof.

2. **HYNSON'S DEPARTMENT STORE**
   9101 Center Street
   This structure reflects the "new" commercial style which evolved after the Great Fire in 1905. Two stories in height, it was constructed circa 1906 of brick with cast stone quoins (decorative blocks on building corners) and lintels (supports above and below windows). The first floor facade features a cast iron storefront, the only one in Manassas. The white specks in the mortar are ground oyster shells which were used as a binding agent for the mortar. All the materials used were thought to be state-of-the-art in fireproof technology for the early twentieth century. In the interior, the pressed steel ceiling (commonly called tin ceiling) features cherubic portraits and is supported by cast—iron columns with Corinthian capitals.

3. **MASONIC LODGE**
   9107 Center Street
   Designed by John Tillett, a local stonemason, and built by local contractor John Cannon circa 1906, this Renaissance Revival building features a hipped roof and originally displayed five arches across the front. Note the Masonic emblem in the upper facade.

4. **HOPKINS CANDY FACTORY**
   9415 Battle Street
   Designed by Manassas architect Albert Speiden and completed in 1908, this three-story structure was reported to be one of the most modern factories in the South. The two-color tone of brick is a common element throughout the downtown. Of particular interest is the decorative cornice constructed on only two sides—the public views from the street and from the railroad tracks. Also note the castellated surround (castle-like outline) of the doorway, which was originally constructed as an arcaded entrance.

5. **HIBBS & GIDDINGS STORE**
   9129 Center Street
   Originally a clothing store owned by E. Humphrey Hibbs and Eugene Giddings, this two-story structure serves as an anchor on this busy corner in the retail district. Notice the exterior steel ceiling, which continues through the leaded glass transom into the interior. This ceiling is supported by columns with Ionic capitals, characterized by the two scroll-like ornaments, or volutes. (Similar ceilings can be found in the Hynson Building as well as Rohr's Store 9122 Center St.) Designed by Manassas architect Albert Speiden, the storefront is unique in Manassas.

6. **PEOPLES NATIONAL BANK**
   9110-9112 Center Street
   Manassas has several of the "corner style" buildings in the Historic District. Built as the Peoples National Bank circa 1904, notable features include grey sandstone quoins and lintels, a molded cornice, and battlements on the parapet. The structure now houses restaurants and shops with apartments above.

7. **HAZEN BUILDING**
   9406 Battle Street
   This commercial building (circa 1875) possesses a strong Italianate influence. A bracketed cornice (where roof meets wall) and projecting hood molds (over the windows) are representative of this style which evolved from the villas of northern Italy, migrated through England, and became popular in this country in the 1860s. The original first-floor display window is typical of the time period, while the intact storefront represents the oldest existing storefront in the Manassas area.

8. **MACBRYDE-WAGENER HOUSE**
   9403 Battle Street
   (private residence)
   Built in the 1890s, this Victorian home has a projecting central pavilion and is an example of the large, comfortable homes built in Manassas as the county seat was established here in 1894. Note the gable-end shutter shaped to fit the arched window. The original owner was W. C. Wagener, a hardware dealer.

9. **ALBERT SPEIDEN HOUSE**
   9320 Battle Street
   (private residence)
   Built and inhabited by one of Manassas's leading architects, this two-story frame residence features a steeply-pitched hipped roof and overhanging eaves. The various angles in the roofline give the house a unique style. The interior features an example of Speiden's design trademark—the water lily—painted in watercolors upon the fireplace's cement facing. A lily is also visible in the stained glass work on the front exterior.

10. **HIXSON-ARLINGTON HOUSE**
    9319 Main Street
    (private residence)
    The original portion of this attractive home was built about 1868 by G. W. Hixson, a member of Mosby's Partisan Rangers. The north wing was added in the late nineteenth century. This example of an "ell house" (house shape similar to the letter "L") features a five bay construction and a standing seam metal roof, often found in Manassas.

11. **9312 MAIN STREET**
    (private residence)
    This American Four Square has a distinct personality as it exhibits Prairie-style windows and eaves and a wraparound porch. Frank Lloyd Wright, the leading architect of Chicago's Prairie School, emphasized a horizontal appearance to complement midwestern terrain. The Prairie influence of this structure traveled east via popular magazines and house catalogues such as *Sears & Roebuck*, *Montgomery Ward*, and *Alladin Homes*.

12. **9306 MAIN STREET**
    (private residence)
    Throughout the period 1908 to 1940, Sears Roebuck & Company sold prefabricated homes from their celebrated catalogue. This is an example of the "Kilbourne" model which sold for around $2,600 in the 1920s. A steeply-pitched gable roof, a dormer, overhanging eaves, exposed rafter tails, and massive porch pillars characterize this bungalow-type structure. This particular model appeared in the Sears catalog from 1921 to 1929.

13. **PORTNER GATEHOUSE**
    9218 Portner Avenue
    (private residence)
    Now a residence, this was the gatehouse to Robert Portner's estate, Annaburg, on Maple Avenue (1892). Note the remnants of the local stone gate posts on the southeast corner of the intersection. Portner's German origin lends a European feel to the Annaburg structures. Note the pyramidal hipped roof and the decorative cornice on this small scale dwelling.

14. **LIBEAU ROW**
    9225 block, Portner Avenue
    (private residence)
    Built by New Zealand emigrant Donation Libeau about 1905, these four T-shaped structures obviously share the same style. The Libeaus also operated a brickyard just south of Manassas. (The first, third, and fourth houses have been painted to compensate for soft brickwork. For similar reasons, the second structure has been stuccoed). These are the only row houses built in Manassas during this time period.

15. **S. T. WEIR HOUSE**
    9313 West Street
    (private residence)
    Built about 1880 by one of the earliest families of Manassas, this home has a bracketed cornice and a projecting dormer with a bull's-eye window. Note the decorative shingles on the dormer. This home compares with the MacBryde-Wagener Home in style and size.

16. **PRINCE WILLIAM COUNTY COURTHOUSE**
    9300 Lee Avenue
    Completed in 1894, the courthouse is a Victorian Romanesque structure built of sandstone and brick, featuring a low-hipped roof, use of Manassas shale in the quoins and lintels, and slender round-headed windows. The prominent wood and metal cupola and clock tower alter the rectangular shape of this building which served as the court until 1984.

CHAPTER 6
MARINES SETTLE ON THE LONG WATER

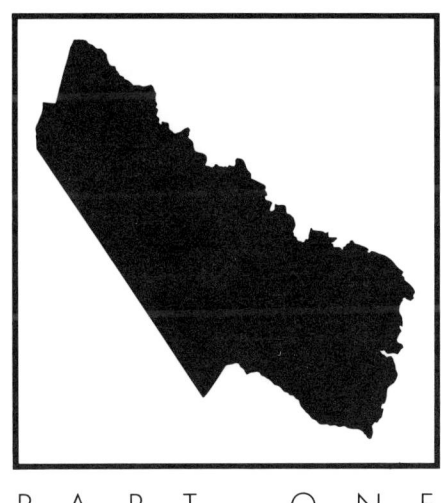

PART ONE

As the United States drew closer to the threshold of participation in World War I, the Marine Corps was told to expand to meet the coming need. The Corps was able to to do this by setting up a separate base, rather than having training facilities on naval bases as was formerly the case. In the spring of 1917, a committee of Marine officers inspected possible sites in the Washington area. They eventually elected to lease fifty-three hundred acres from a financially troubled company which had been trying to develop a peninsula south of the federal city. It was known locally as Quantico, for the stream that emptied into the Potomac in that area. Quantico is an Indian word meaning "the long water." There was an officially incorporated town called Potomac, a shipyard, a small hotel, and some cottages that had been built to draw vacationers. In late April 1917, the lease from the Potomac Company was approved; instead of a riverside playground for vacationers, Quantico became the training area for seven thousand Marines bound for the trenches in France.

Fifty years later in May 1967, some of the survivors had a reunion and reminisced. "Quantico," said L. Paul Taylor, "was hot as a pistol and muddier than a pigsty." There weren't enough barracks, so the troops slept on and under an outdoor dance pavilion. For awhile they did their laundry in the river, added retired Brig. Gen. William F. Brown. But Taylor emphasized they were not unhappy— because they were doing their duty. In those days to be a slacker was to be despised.

Even with the government payments, the Quantico Company was hard pressed. In December 1917, the company offered to sell the leased land to the Marines for half a million dollars, a proposition which was accepted.

Marine aviation came to Quantico in 1919 with the arrival of Aviation Squadron C, fresh from France. By 1922, two airfields had been built, one west of the tracks and one on the east, jutting into the Potomac. Both were named for Lt. Walter Brown, a Marine aviator killed in a plane crash there in 1921. Brown had been a star quarterback on the Marine team that played in the Rose Bowl in 1918. This is the view of Brown field in 1931, when the Marines were constructing a new, less hazardous field inland. To do this they rerouted Chopawamsic Creek and drained the swamp. The second field was dedicated in 1936 and named in honor of Col. Thomas C. Turner, killed in Haiti in 1931.

Maj. Gen. John Lejeune assumed command at Quantico in 1919. General Lejeune believed that military training should not occupy the whole day, and inaugurated other studies for half of the workday. After a battalion of Marines that was shipped to the Caribbean in mid-course on the Henderson *asked to be allowed to continue their studies, subjects were prepared to be sent by mail. Thus began the oldest correspondence school in the armed forces.*

These Marine Corps language students look almost modern with their earphones, becoming accustomed to the sound as well as the sight of foreign words. Spanish and French both would have been useful to men with a good chance of drawing duty in Haiti and Central America. The United States attempted to deal with unrest by sending in the Marines to restore and maintain order far more than is usually remembered. The Fifteenth Regiment of Marines from Quantico landed in Santo Domingo in 1919. The First Marine Brigade spent nineteen years in neighboring Haiti, while other detachments put in almost the identical amount of time in Nicaragua. The Sandinista party in Nicaragua of the 1980s is named for a revolutionary leader, Sandino, who was operating when the Fifth Marine Regiment from Quantico was in Nicaragua from 1927 to 1933.

This view of Quantico in 1926 shows a town which had returned to prewar occupations of commercial fishing and selling timber. After Quantico became incorporated again in 1928, Prohibition triggered a confrontation with the Marine command. Maj. Gen. Smedley D. Butler boycotted the town until the merchants stopped the sale of illegal whiskey. Someone, General Butler said forecefully "had been loading up my boys with bootleg poison." Once the moonshiners left the vicinity, the town and corps were able to co-exist in relative calm.

Far from fighting the last war, as military leaders are sometimes accused of doing, throughout the 1930s the Marine high command was preparing for the amphibious war to come in the Pacific. Part of this training included land maneuvers, sending Marine detachments over dusty trails as far west as the Bull Run Mountains. Like this group, they found many streams still had fords, not bridges; permission to cross a farmer's land included the promise to close all the gates behind them.

The Marines were probably the first Civil War re-enactors. In 1924, three thousand of them marched all the way from Quantico to Sharpsburg, Maryland, to recreate the Battle of Antietam. As early as 1921 they restaged the Battle of the Wilderness southwest of Fredericksburg; in 1923 they took on the Virginia Military Institute cadets in a reenactment of the Battle of New Market in the Shenandoah Valley.

World War II poster
Posters and photographs are courtesy of the
U.S. Marine Corps Archives

Very near the site of the Dairy Festival, within the city limits of Manassas, stood Clover Hill, a two hundred-year-old dairy farm, still owned by the descendents of Rutland Johnson who bought it in 1770. The family finally sold the land to a developer in 1988.
Courtesy of Marianna Durst

Pre-World War II Prince William

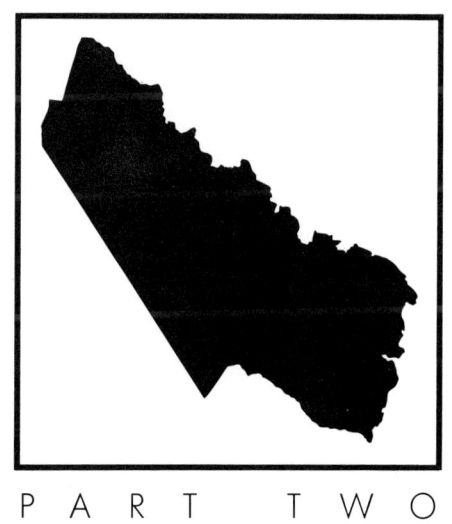

PART TWO

The grand finale of the Dairy Festival was a parade and the crowning of the queen. This took place on the grounds of Annaburg, the Portner estate in Manassas.
Courtesy of the Manassas City Museum

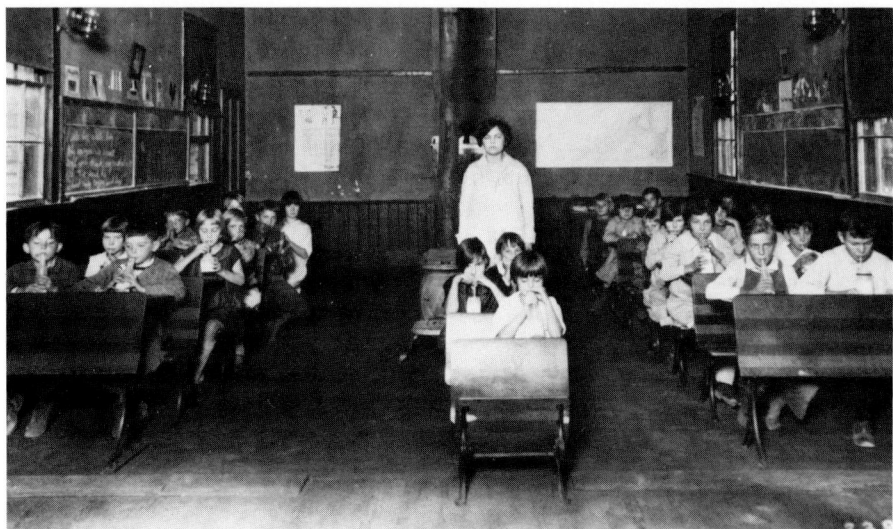

Everyone supported the festival advertising campaign. These conscientious milk drinkers went to a one-room school as did many scholars in Prince William County in the 1930s.
Courtesy of Hattie Mae Partlow

A major source of farm income in Prince William County in the twentieth century was milk products. They were shipped to Washington by train. In 1920 the dairy farmers of Maryland and Virginia banded together to form the Milk Producers Association. Through their combined effort they were able to steady seasonally fluctuating prices, ensure uniform quality, and achieve other goals it would have been hard for them to do as individuals. One hundred and twenty farmers from Prince William belonged to the association.

To further assist this cause, a group of Manassas businessmen joined with a group of dairymen to organize the Piedmont Dairy Festival. This was an annual celebration which promoted dairy products. Eleven counties participated in the festival. The first Piedmont Dairy Festival was held in 1931, the last in 1937.[1]

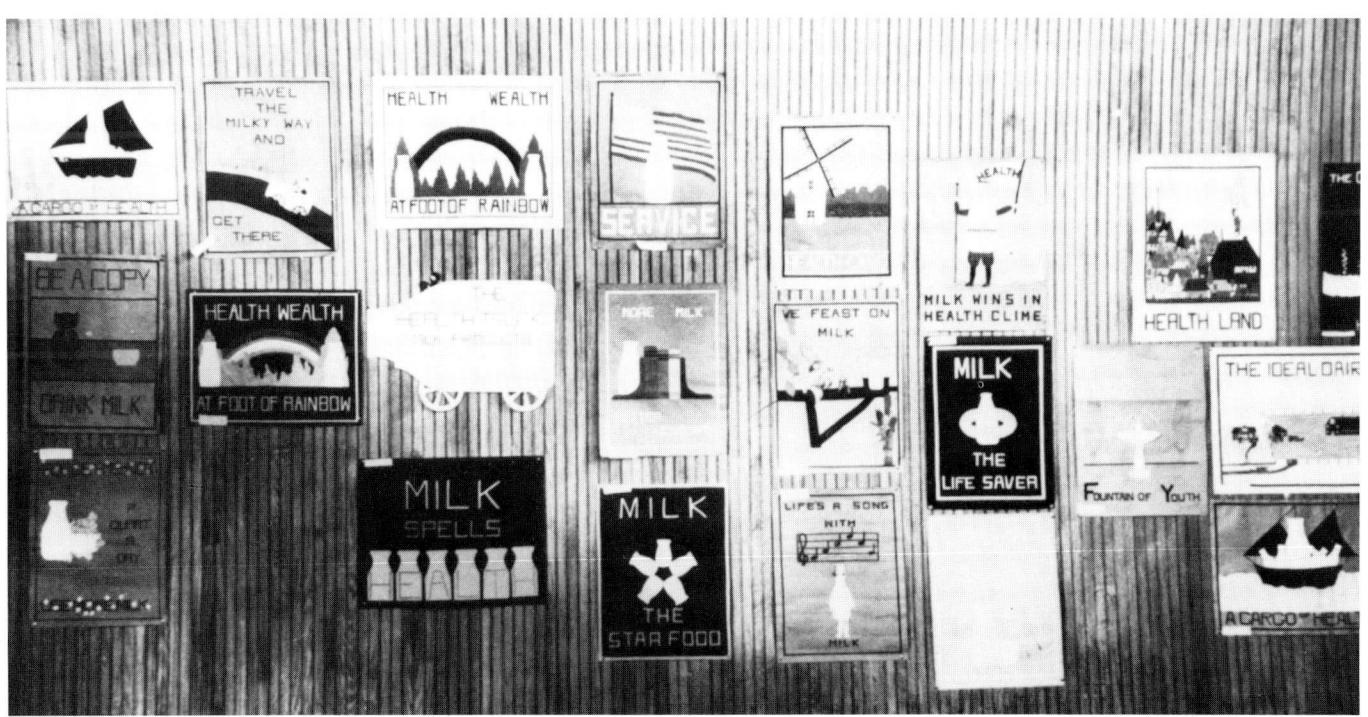

This is Catharpin School, another of the many that still dotted the rural landscape in the Dairy Festival days. It was built in 1898 with just one room, that on the right.
Courtesy of Marianna Durst

Posters were another creative outlet for dairy promotion.
Courtesy of the Manassas City Museum

Meanwhile the sources of production were enjoying green pastures. This herd was in western Prince William.
Courtesy of Hattie Mae Partlow

Contented dairy cows graze at Mountain View Farm, a home built by one of the Carter heirs on the lower Bull Run tract, still intact in 1936.
Courtesy of the Manassas National Battlefield Park

Yet another development of the 1930s was the appearance of district high schools. High school education was not taken for granted by all in those days, and the enrollment was often so small the authorities debated the financial feasibility of continuing. Shown here is the first graduating class of Brentsville District High in Nokesville, the class of 1930.
From The Flash, *yearbook[2].*

In this twenty-fifth anniversary edition of The Flash, *the Brentsville District High School yearbook, the senior class reflects a time of traditional values and relative prosperity.*
Courtesy of Hattie Mae Partlow

Brentsville District High was the first in the county to have the music training necessary for a school band and chorus. Their parents paid the teacher and held fundraisers to buy them second-hand uniforms. After the band's first concert performance at rival Manassas City High, that high school lobbied to have music in its curriculum. The school board acquiesced at least in the hiring of a qualified teacher, with the stipulation the music teacher must also teach academic subjects.
Courtesy of Hattie Mae Partlow

First principal of Brentsville District High was C. O. Bittle. There were eighty-eight students in grades 1 through 11 when the school opened in the fall of 1929.
From The Flash *yearbook of 1955*

This was Manassas City High which began in 1925 and stood next to Bennett School, across from the present Judicial Center. In 1935 the name was changed to Osbourn High, and in 1982 the building was torn down. The other district high school, covering the eastern section of the county was in Occoquan.
Courtesy of Hattie Mae Partlow

Many little villages had sprung up in Prince William County to meet the needs of enclaves of farm folk. Before the advent of rural free delivery (RFD), such hamlets existed where the farmers picked up mail and supplies. They served as natural locations for churches and schools as well. This is the old post office at Waterfall, located near the place where Catharpin Run comes down from the Bull Run Mountains into the stream of the same name. The man on the bicycle was Fred Leppert. Catharpin provided power for a number of mills. According to former residents, the workers of a logging mill generated business for a number of saloons in the village. An atmosphere of general chaos was created on Saturday nights and the morning after, not only in the village but on the roads leading there.[3]
Courtesy of Pauline Padgett

Many villages are being enveloped by the suburbs in modern Prince William. Here and there a landmark falls prey to the ravages of time and disappears. One such was Bacon Race Church in the area known as Hoadley in the northeastern section of the county. It was built about 1880 by a congregation of "Hard Shelled" Baptists. In 1987, preservationists were working to save the building, but a severe storm hastened its collapse.
Courtesy of Marianna Durst

Another church not far away from Bacon Race was more fortunate. This is Bethel Church, as it looked in 1940, standing near the intersection of Smoketown and Davis Ford roads. The church was the nucleus for the village called Bethel. In 1977, when the church was threatened with demolition by the highway department, a group of its new neighbors contributed five thousand dollars and a considerable amount of labor to move the old church. The Methodist congregation had just paid for a new building and could not afford to move the old one.

Bethel Church was built in 1850 on land donated by the Glasscocks. Like most county churches, it served as a hospital during the Civil War and needed renovation afterwards.[4]

Courtesy of the Bethel Historical Society

Summertime brought Vacation Bible School for the Bethel congregation in June 1949. With apologies to those who were not identified, they are, top row, left to right: Medrith Garber, Rev. Clark Wood, and Lucy Puffenbarger. Row two: David Collins Glasscock, Virginia Sullivan, Frances Ann Garner, Hazel Saunders, Ione Glasscock, Irene Mottl, Anna Mae Summerville, Betty Ilse, Virgie Hedges, Ollie Furr, and Jeanette Garber. Row three: Janice Thurston, Betty Cornell, Martha Anne Puffenbarger, Dickie Mottl, Nancy Harold, Jean Crummett, Dorothy Thorpe, Christine Tillyer, Frances Carney, Orma Jean Wolfrey, unknown, Nancy Clinedinst, Herbert Crummett, Wiidrow Able, Thelma Cornell, Polly Thurston, Nelva Jean Moon, Joan Thurston, Urple Fair, and a granddaughter of Reverend Wood (name unknown). Row four: Rosie Able, Sybil Rigney, Pauline Mitchell, Emma Cornell, Donna Carney, Helen Crummett, Sandy Mitchell, Donnie Hull, Edward Thorpe, Faye Best, Ruth Cornell, Betty Mosser, Dorothy May Hale, Hoberta Sommerville, Betty Jean Ilse, Charles Simmons, Adeline Crummett, Alice Moon, Bobby Furr, and Leon Hull. Row five: Junior Simmons, unknown, Virginia Weeks, Ralph Clinedinst, ___ Thorpe, Carol Clinedinst, Bobby Best, Roger Puffenbarger, Shirley Puffenbarger, Michael Garber, Wayne Mosser, Charlotte Mosser, Wayne White, Gary Mottl, unknown, unknown, Janna Lee Murphy, Neil Garber, unknown, Bobby Ilse, and ___ Weekes.

Courtesy of the Bethel Historical Society

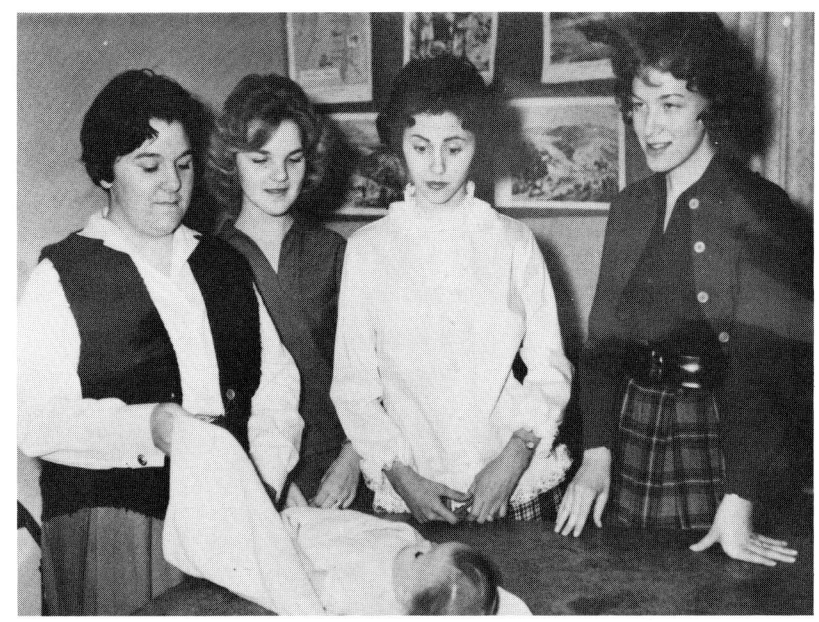

Churches like Bethel which were community centers, could be 4-H Club meeting places as demonstrated in this 1961 photo of a child care class. From left to right: Brenda Palmer, Louise Johnson, Shirley Puffenbarger, and Janna Lee Murphy. Courtesy of the Bethel Historical Society

Here Bethel is shown fulfilling its community center function as the scene of an open air political rally on July 11, 1959. The speaker was Judge William May. To his immediate left, seated, in a light colored suit, was G. C. Russell, a leading citizen of the area, active in Democratic party politics. The man to Judge May's right is a Mr. Gallagher. Courtesy of the Bethel Historical Society

Another landmark at Bethel, which stood not far from the church, was the home of Mr. and Mrs. G. C. Russell. The Russells bought the home in 1917. The central portion of the house is believed to have been built around a house shown on that site on an 1848 plat. Russell had a store next to his house, seen in the background. The house and store are likely to be demolished soon by road widening activities.

For a number of years, probably from the 1920s through the 1950s, Russell owned a hog farm, managed for him by the Garber family. In the 1940s the hogs numbered thirty-five hundred, forming the largest hog farm in the area. The proliferation of hog farms occurred up and down the East Coast near large cities, because hogs could be fed with the table scraps from restaurants and hotels. According to Galen Garber, the laws which required first that the restauranteurs refrigerate the garbage before pickup, and later, required the farmers to steam sterilize it before feeding the hogs, made hog farming become an onerous and expensive business. Garber helped his father manage the Russell farm and later had a hog farm of his own. Courtesy of Janna Murphy Leepson

Charles Green and his family used this large, beautiful house, The Lawn, as a summer residence in the late nineteenth century. Two of his grandchildren, a brother and sister raised in Paris, wrote of the days when this picture was taken, about 1880, drawing on stories their parents had told them.

"The Greens alighted (from the train) at Nokesville to be met by a crowd of relatives and friends. All the family lived at The Lawn in summer with consorts and children. One of Edward's (Anne and Julian's father) sisters was married, the others reveled in beaux, looks, high spirits, and Paris clothes. From the station, the men rode while women and children drove in buggies drawn by nervous, prancing horses. Away they went, over the worst roads in the world. The carts plunged through shallow creeks, or when a boulder barred the way, the corduroy lane divided and it was skirted.... nothing is of much importance when you own the hard red soil, the poor crops, the closely planted woods, a distant view of the Blue Ridge foothills, the delicious hum and haze of summer and have no cares, nothing but love and gaiety .... The house is filled with quick footsteps, bursts of laughter as a door opens, scurrying of little feet, exchanges of visits and always that talking, talking of Southern life as though there weren't words enough to tell one another all about nothing...the children, sitting at supper, raised wondering heads at the continuous revelry of the big folks."[4]

Anne Green journeyed all the way from France in 1920 to see the home where her expatriate parents had spent such happy vacations, early in their marriage. The night before she was to arrive, The Lawn burned to the ground, to remain always for her a mirage of memory.

Her brother Julian, considered a contender at one time for the Nobel prize in literature, opened his Harper award-winning autobiography with a recollection: "Both my parents were Southerners. My mother came from Savannah, Georgia, and my father from Prince William County, Virginia. When my mother felt combative, she would taunt my father with the fact that Virginia was the last state to secede and my elder sisters would say: 'There they go again!'"[5]

From the collection of James Cooke

Greenwich

PART THREE

No one knows who named this centuries-old crossroads village for the home of the prime meridian. It was called Greenwich in Revolutionary times when Hessian soldiers marched by Thornton's Tavern (shown here) on their way to a prisoner of war camp in Charlottesville. Thomas Thornton was one of the first resident landowners in the area, and although he left before the eighteenth century was over, his house figures in old deeds and descriptions as Thornton's Tavern. An English traveler, writing in the early nineteenth century, noted that inns in America "had no sign but take their name from the person who keeps the house, who is often a man of consequence."[1] In the nineteenth century, the former tavern became the estate manager's house for The Lawn. It was razed in 1973.
From the collection of James Cooke

Greenwich, like most other Northern Virginia hamlets and towns of the early twentieth century, had its own baseball team. This is the 1915 team which upheld the honor of the village in contests with Haymarket, The Plains, Warrenton, and others nearby. Bottom row, left to right: John Ellis, Will Ritenour; second row, left to right, Raymond Ellis, Ernest Reid, Frank Cockrell, and Dan House; back row, left to right, Rob McClearn, Walter House and Tom Thornton.
From the collection of James Cooke

Greenwich Presbyterian Church is the most notable landmark where the old Mountain Road from the coast crosses the detour the Indians made in their Carolina Road.[2] The first church on the site was a little log cabin, built in 1810 when the living room at The Grove could no longer hold the Presbyterian meetings. It was begun by Aminta Douglass, a Marylander who moved to Virginia after her marriage to Gilbert Ireland Moxley of Greenwich in 1802. In 1812 a frame church superceded the log edifice, and was in use until 1858.

In that year, just before Aminta Moxley's death, the brick church was built through the generosity of one of her granddaughters, Lucy Ireland Hunton of Buckland, who had married a wealthy Englishman and a cotton broker, Charles Green from Savannah. Green is credited with saving the church from destruction by Union troops during the Civil War. He intervened, presenting himself as the citizen of a neutral nation, claiming the church as his property because it would revert or "drawback" to him if it were used for other than religious purposes.[3]
From the collection of James Cooke

Oakdale Baptist Church, which is situated on the Old Carolina Road detour, began in 1860 when a congregation formed under the leadership of the Reverend B. P. Dulin. Meetings were held in a tent at that time and suffered a hiatus during the Civil War. The first building was erected about 1870, and served until replaced by another frame church built in 1912. The church in use today was finished in 1960.
From the collection of James Cooke

Like other villages also, Greenwich had its general store, the gathering place for wit and wisdom and news and just visiting. This 1918 crowd at Woods Store, which stood next to Mayhughs on Route 215, includes, from left to right: Malcolm Washington, Epp Allen, Murray Leach, Ben Wood, Beverly Leach, Henry Wood, Wallace Wood, Elias Brooks, and Will Dodd. Although he seems a personable hound, the dog's name has been forgotten.
From the collection of James Cooke

This building was known as The Old Red School, although it began as an Episcopal mission church, called Sunnyside by the three Englishmen who built it. In the latter half of the nineteenth century, however, there were not enough Anglicans to support a church in the sparsely populated district. The building was therefore sold to the Prince William County School Board to become the first public school in Greenwich under the Constitution of 1870. From the collection of James Cooke

*The children in the picture are of both the classes at the first Greenwich school built as such. It was built about 1903, but is no longer standing. Bottom row, left to right: Harry House, unknown, Raymond Ellis, Harry Riley, Chub Bell, Joe Wood (partially obscured), Oakley Taylor, Robert Kidwell, Frank Cockrell, Jim House, and Rod McClearn. Second row: Carol House, Oscar Riley, Dossie Riley, May House, Mae Taylor, Anna Mayhugh, George Risdon, Mackall Ellis, Doug Cockrell, John Ellis, Hunton Washington, and Charlie Wood. Third row: Unknown, Lulu Mayhugh (hat), Elnora Bell, May Cooke, Katie Kidwell, Annie Taylor, Mamie Nalls, Louise Kidwell, Mary Dulin, Mary Cockrell, and Katie Boley (white dress). Fourth row: Janie Herrell (teacher), Lucy Taylor (with beads), Mamie Jones (big hat), Jerry Brown, Katie Cockrell (big hat), Lena House, Will Blackwell (teacher), George Wood, and Elese Dulin. Top row: (3 boys) Will Armstrong, Shirley Risdon, and Unknown. Note several of the littlest boys on the front row are shown at a later age on the 1915 baseball team.
From the collection of James Cooke*

A graphic example of attrition through lack of ownership is shown here in the Willoughby Tebbs house, a Georgian home in Dumfries, also used briefly as the county court while the permanent building was being built. This photograph of the unoccupied house was taken after the 1933 storm which inflicted so much damage the building had to be razed in 1934. The sagging floor was of an unusual type called a Carcase Floor, which had a triple system of structural members. Only the inside paneling and woodwork had been saved by a New York firm and put in a building in that city.
Courtesy of the Library of Congress, from the Frances Benjamin Johnston Carnegie Survey

As The Past Serves The Present

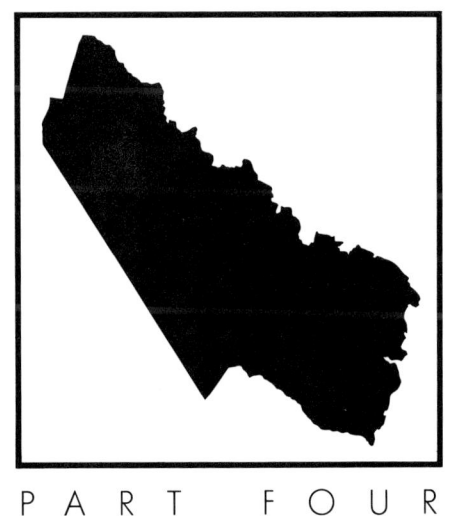

PART FOUR

Fortunately at that time two other eighteenth-century buildings in the town were being put to what today is called "adaptive use." They had been turned into boarding houses. Officers from the nearby Marine base at Quantico were most in need of such facilities, but school teachers and ministers were also made welcome. This is Henderson House as it looked in 1913 when Dr. David C. Cline bought it. The house had been vacant and vandalized for years. It had served as shelter for vagrants, whose trash filled the premises. Annie Keys Cline, formerly of "Cedar Hill" farm, was not overly optimistic about her husband's purchase. Dr. Cline came to northern Virginia from West Virginia in 1905. He saw the potential in the old house and set up his medical office downstairs after the restoration. Henderson House was probably built prior to 1785 when Alexander Henderson moved his mercantile operations over from Colchester and took up residence. His son, Archibald, who lived here as a child, became the fifth commandant of the U.S. Marine Corps, and still holds the record for the longest assignment in the job, from 1820 to 1859.[1]

Another restoration on Henderson House is presently being done by the Clines' grandson, who found a plastered over window in the wall between the hall and the living room. This indicates a probable double house, the earliest portion of which was one room over one room, perhaps during the beginning days of the port of Dumfries. The road running past the front door was the route from Dumfries to the Blue Ridge Mountains. Now starting a short distance north it is known as Route 234.
Courtesy of Christopher Brown

Annie Cline Shumate, granddaughter of Magruder and Annie McCracken Keys, lived in Henderson House for almost seventy-nine years. When her first husband, Dr. Cline, died in 1931, she rearranged and added rooms for rental apartments. She became a member of the Prince William County School Board in 1920, and over a period of years she was instrumental in helping start four elementary schools and Occoquan District High School.

In 1932, she married the Rev. Albert H. Shumate, who had rented a room from the Clines in 1921, when he first came to Dumfries to teach after his graduation from Randolph-Macon College in Ashland, Virginia.
Courtesy of Christopher Brown

The strictures of economics have often obliged the citizens of Prince William to stand by sadly while landmarks of the past vanished before their eyes. Fire has also destroyed much—a great portion of eighteenth-century Dumfries in the first quarter of the nineteenth century, the Lee home on Leesylvania not long after the Revolution, the famous Merchants' Mill of Thomas Ellicott in 1924. For whatever reason, much has gone that could still be used today were it still here.

In this 1930s postcard, saved by a former owner, the inn was enjoying a rebirth in the motor age. The porches added during that era have since disappeared. So has the prosperity, eroded by the construction of the modern super highway, now Interstate 95, which siphoned off the traffic and bypassed the village.
Courtesy of Hilary Costello

Although the hotel business declined, there were still customers for rented rooms, but even that dwindled as the expense of maintenance proved too much for the owner. In 1972 Hilary Costello, Dumfries councilman and a member of Historic Dumfries, bought the eighteenth-century ordinary. His son Brad stands in front of the fireplace, which once warmed the persons of such luminaries as George Mason and George Washington. Previous owners had relocated the front hall staircase and converted the upstairs to a number of small bedrooms for twentieth-century occupancy. Studs are still visible in the upstairs hall floor for the walls of two large dormitory-like rooms, the eighteenth-century way of providing sleeping accomodation.
Courtesy of Hilary Costello

Brad's brother Steve Costello does his share of digging out the basement, during his summer vacation from Virginia Military Institute in 1988, a chore which yielded several two-hundred-year old wine bottles. Three sides of the house are done in Flemish bond; the side facing the highway is laid in a rare "all headers" pattern. In the side wall, seen in this picture, there are occasional decorative bands of headers.
Courtesy of the author

There is nothing left of the third Prince William County Court House at Dumfries, but the court house built at Brentsville between 1820 and 1822 is still standing. Seen here in the 1950s, it served the surrounding farm community as a meeting place, but the burden of maintenance was proving too great. Today it is the home of the Prince William County Historical Commission.
Courtesy of Marianna Durst

Across the county road from the Brentsville court house is a structure known as "The White House." In 1939, when it attracted the attention of Agnes Webster and her husband, who were looking for a country home to replace their Alexandria house. The White House had not been lived in for ten years.
Courtesy of Agnes Webster

The cornfield behind The White House might seem to suggest this was once a farm, but that is deceptive. The house was built in 1822 by John Williams, the clerk of the court at the time the court was moved from Dumfries, and the new town was chartered by legislature.
Courtesy of Agnes Webster

Inside the building was not much better. The bank officer who came out to investigate the Webster's candidate for a loan would not let his wife inside the house. He was afraid one of the walls might fall on her. The plastering was all redone, not patched, but the new owners were able to save the original woodwork in the house. Courtesy of Agnes Webster

When the Websters finished restoring "The White House," they moved into it and began living there during World War II. Of course, the village square, the hotels, and much of the population of its days as a county seat were gone, but there still was a village in 1939. The Websters' son attended the one-room school and they did much of their shopping at the general store. They went to dances in the old court house. Agnes Webster remembers the neighbors bringing little bundled up babies and laying them in rows along the wall to sleep while their parents danced. The courthouse, as a community center, was also available for service projects such as bake sales and club meetings. Eventually the upkeep for the community center became too much for the neighborhood, and the county was persuaded to take over the upkeep and use it for a Park System office. Courtesy of Agnes Webster

Perhaps one of the most interesting and encouraging stories of historic preservation concerns the only riverside plantation home still standing, Rippon Lodge, built by Richard Blackburn about 1725. In 1924 it was noised about in Dumfries by Tom and Gus Marion, brothers living in Rippon Lodge and doing some farming on the old plantation, that Rippon Lodge had been bought by Judge Wade Hampton Ellis.

What the people of Dumfries may not have known at first was that Judge Ellis, shown here with his wife, was related to Richard Blackburn through his mother, Kate Blackburn Ellis. When Prince William County had its two hundredth birthday in 1931, Judge Ellis served as chairman of the celebration.[2]
Courtesy of Ellis Hawkins

*Although Colonial Williamsburg scouts had bid for the paneling in the dining room at the lodge, the men living there had declined to sell this reminder of the inside of a seventeenth-century manor house recreated in America. Instead, Judge Ellis hired Elvan Keys and his crew of Dumfries carpenters to return the house as nearly as possible to its eighteenth-century size and character. The men reported they found evidence of the early foundations as they added two rooms, one on either end.[3]
Courtesy of the Library of Congress*

*In 1928, the restoration complete, Judge Ellis hired a Marylander, Edward Hawkins, to live on the former plantation and manage it for him. Hawkins is shown here with the combination lawnmower-roller, which was used to keep the estate like a park, with bridle paths ready for Judge Ellis and his friends to go for a canter at any time. This provided full-time work for five or six men during the Depression of the 1930s. The surrounding woods served to supply firewood for the Lodge, the homes of the staff, the Ellis' home on Massachusetts Avenue in the District of Columbia, and the homes of several widows in Dumfries as well.
Courtesy of Ellis Hawkins*

*Edward Hawkins, shown with his wife, Alice, and sons, Cleggett (left) and Ellis (right) managed one thousand acres on either side of Route 1 for Judge Ellis from 1928 until Mr. Hawkins' death in 1948. Cleggett became a Navy pilot and died during World War II. Ellis graduated from Occoquan District High and has worked for Virginia Power since 1948. From 1969 to 1977 he served on the Prince William County School Board. From 1972 to 1976 he was its chairman.
Courtesy of Ellis Hawkins*

Meanwhile, half a world away, another of Richard Blackburn's descendents was mapping the coast of Antarctica for Admiral Byrd, administering Trust territories for the United States and, as a consequence, waiting on Howland Island for Amelia Earhart when she disappeared on her round the world flight. This portrait of Rear Adm. Richard Blackburn Black was painted by Helena Urgenyi Breunay after his stint with the second Byrd expedition to the South Pole in 1933 to 1935.
Courtesy of Rear Admiral and Mrs. R. B. Black

Captain Black, as he was then, returned from his second trip to Antarctica (1939 to 1941) in time to be recalled to active duty with the Navy. He lived on the shore of Pearl Harbor on December 7, 1941. Shown here with his wife, Avisa, and son, Douglas, whose mother, Black's first wife, died while he was on his first trip to Antarctica.
Courtesy of Rear Admiral and Mrs. R. B. Black

Rear Admiral Black grew up in Grand Forks, North Dakota—good training, he observed, for surveying at the South Pole by dog sled and on skis. Five hundred miles of the coast of Antarctica bear his name: he named a mountain that reminded him of a three-cornered hat, the Tricorne Mountain. Until 1965, however, he had never actually gotten to ninety-degrees South, the Pole itself. In this U.S. Navy photograph taken that year, he is standing at the South Pole, holding the flag of the Society of the Cincinnati, as if to demonstrate that the descendents of Washington's officer corps are still a part of the action.[4]
Courtesy of Rear Admiral and Mrs. R. B. Black

Since the Blacks' return to Rippon Lodge, another famous explorer has claimed a spot on the wall. Mrs. Black is justly proud of her own fifth great-grandfather, western pioneer Daniel Boone. This portrait of him and his dog Blue was reportedly done about 1818, shortly before he died, by itinerant artist Jean Francois Valle.
Courtesy of Rear Admiral and Mrs. R. B. Black

*In 1952 Rear Admiral Black brought his family to Washington where he joined the staff of the Office of Naval Research. Judge Ellis' widow had just sold Rippon Lodge. When she heard Admiral Black wished to buy the property because it had belonged to his ancestor, she asked the other buyer if he would release her from the contract and let the Admiral buy it, which he did.
Courtesy of Rear Admiral and
Mrs. R. B. Black*

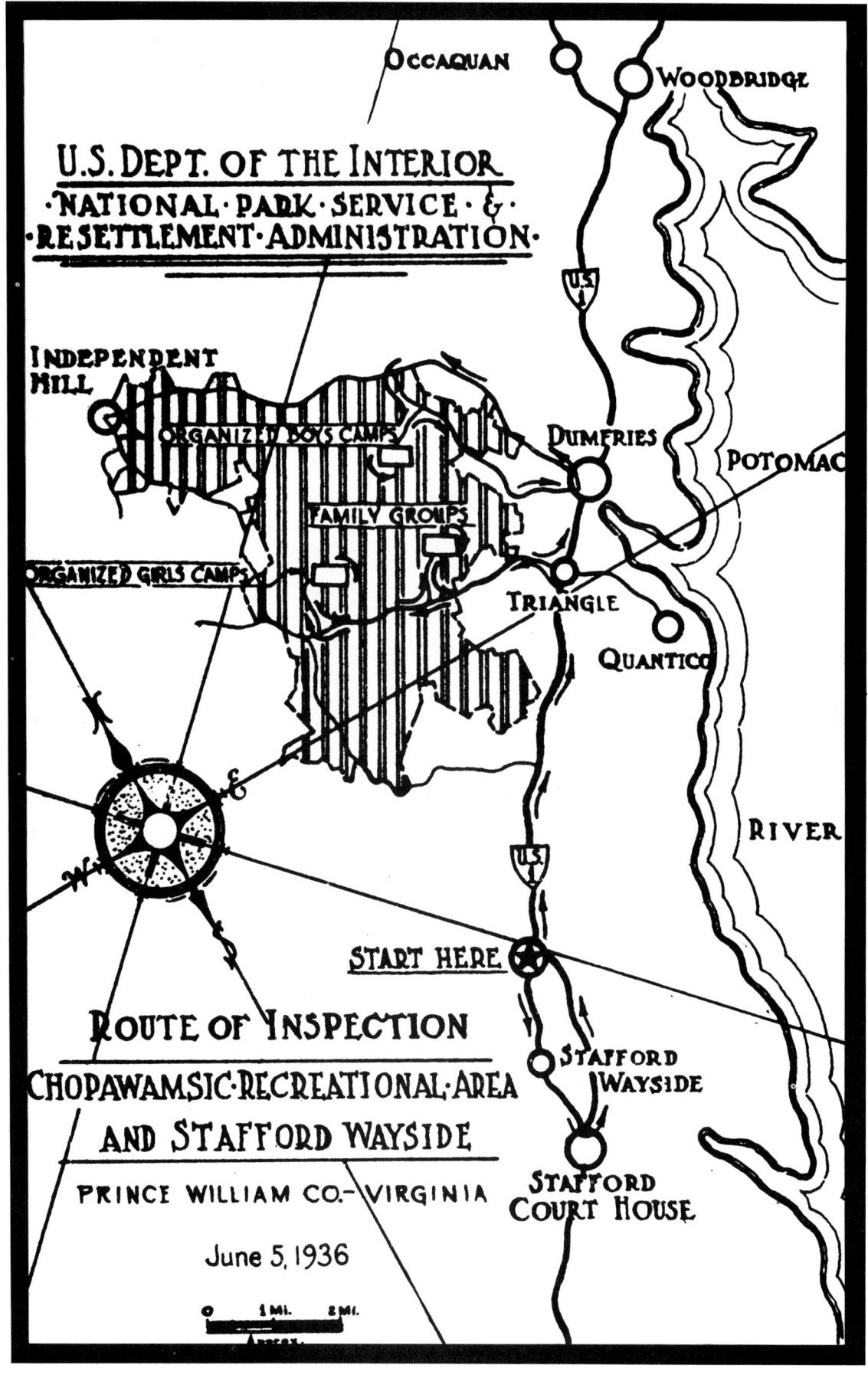

CHAPTER 7
A NEW DEAL FOR PRINCE WILLIAM— CHOPAWAMSIC RDA

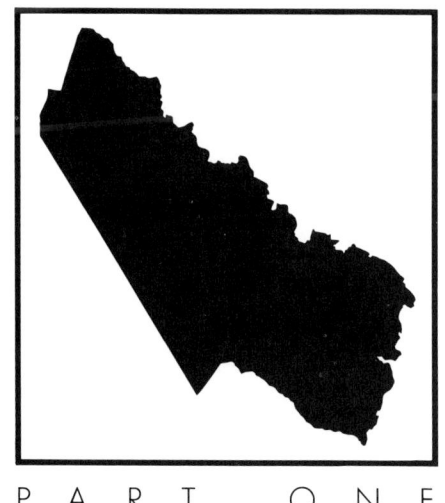

PART ONE

A NEW DEAL

Even today there are some who contest the validity of the premise that created Prince William Forest Park. But if they are a generation removed from those whose land was preempted, they express only a tepid conviction. They would not turn the clock back and return to that precarious existence.

The park was begun as a Recreation Demonstration Area (RDA) during President Franklin D. Roosevelt's first administration. In the depths of the Depression of the 1930s, the RDAs were one means by which the president's economic advisers hoped to relieve poverty both in the city and the country. Across the nation, in farm states suffering special hardship, the Federal Emergency Relief Administration (FERA), headed by Harry L. Hopkins, searched for areas of submarginal land to buy and use as vacation parks for city dwellers who needed vacations, but could not afford them. When the planners found a severely depressed farm area, such as Prince William Forest Park was at that time, the government would buy the land from the owners. If the owners wished to try farming elsewhere, the FERA would help them resettle on better land, or the agency would offer aid in finding alternate occupations.

Because social service agencies in Washington, D.C., asked to have such properties nearby, two of the RDAs were located near the nation's capital—in Catoctin, Maryland, and Chopawamsic, Virginia. These two, unlike most of the RDAs, were not turned back to the states, but were kept as a part of the National Capital Area Park System, administered by the National Park Service.[1]

The federal government spent sixty-six thousand dollars in the acquisition of the fifteen thousand acres that they named the Chopawamsic RDA, commemorating one of the creeks within the recreation project's original boundaries. Scholars believe the name Chopawamsic—"by the separation of the outlet"—originally referred to an Indian village located on or near the delta which causes the creek to have two mouths where it empties into the Potomac.[2]

A final facet of the RDA program was protection and conservation of forest lands. The proposal, using the Prince William County project as an example, reported the area to be an ideal target for conservation of forest lands. As the capstone of the area's suitability for use by city vacationers, the writer added, "Poison ivy is extremely rare."[3]

Before settling upon a given locale for its program to transform farmland into a recreation center, the Department of Interior checked with the local authorities for the area which met the criteria. Prince William County authorities gave Interior officials a bleak picture of the future park region. Very few families living there had steady sources of income; thirty farms had been abandoned or foreclosed for unpaid debt; storekeepers had lost their businesses from overextension of credit; and over 22 percent of the park area residents were delinquent in their tax payments. The area, so the historian reported, probably never had enjoyed sustained prosperity, beginning with the days of tobacco monoculture two hundred years before when the topsoil ran down the hillsides and silted up Quantico Creek.[4]

*Cedar Hill Farm was inherited by a son of Magruder and Annie Keys, Evandon George Washington Keys, born on the first president's birthday in the midst of the Civil War. He married Hannah Elmirah Liming, whose family had moved to the nearby hamlet of Cold Plains (later Joplin) from Asbury, New Jersey, after the war. The Keys sold Cedar Hill Farm and moved to Cold Plains after their children were born. The early land grant apparently had failed to provide the family with permanent rights of way for access roads. Circa 1901 in the back row, left to right: Vanetta Mary, Ruth L. Owen, Eunice L., Annie G., Katie, and Paul Reid. Middle row: Hannah Keys, William Francis, and E. G. W. Keys. Front row: James Isaac and Elvan F.
Courtesy of Hilda Cline Brown Ammerman*

This is one of the farmhomes that stood within the park. Of its former owners, Department of Interior investigators noted that "heads of most of the families, of early American descent, bear their wants and privations through to exhaustion."[5] The Washington Star *echoed this in a story about the proposed recreation area, published March 6, 1935, stating, "Yet because of a deep-seated pride and independence of spirit, very few of the families have applied for relief, despite their poor living conditions."
Courtesy of the Prince William Forest Park*

The Taylor family, shown here on their way to church, lived within the Park bounds until 1939. Robert Taylor, the father, born in 1867, is driving. With him are his wife, Jennie; daughter, Estelle; and son (John) Woodrow, perched in what looks like an early equivalent of a car seat on the floor. Like most Park area families of the time, Taylor supplemented the food he grew to feed his family by working at the Cabin Branch Mine, running a store, and selling timber from the hillside for railroad ties and pulpwood. Woodrow remembered his father as one who "was always looking for ways to improve."
Courtesy of the Prince William Forest Park

Annie Williams, and her five children, lived on Hickory Ridge in the bounds of the RDA. Her second husband, Warfield Kendall, had died in 1934, the year before the government pre-empted her house and land for two thousand dollars. Williams and her second husband came from a long line of free blacks to whom land ownership was especially significant. This picture was taken at her seventy-fifth birthday party twenty years ago. Left to right, Norman Henderson, Bertie Henderson Kyer, Cleve Henderson, Annie Williams, Provie Henderson, and Charles Frank Kendall. Williams' first husband, Robert Henderson, died in the flu epidemic of 1918. She has been married to her third husband, Milton E. Williams since 1944.[6]
Courtesy of Annie Williams

Nancy Simms Thomas

In nearby Minnieville where she grew up, and on Hickory Ridge, a mixed community of blacks and whites, people of both races helped each other when in need, Williams said. It was one of the reasons country folk survived hard times. Her parents, George W. and Nancy Simms Thomas, used up most of the food they grew to feed their family, but they were always prepared to feed neighbors in need, of either race, and often did. Not all the children stayed in Prince William. Her sister, Anita Thomas Triplett, sent home this photograph from Alexandria where she had gone to work.
Courtesy of Annie Williams

George W. Thomas

Anita Thomas Triplett

The Cabin Branch Mine, within the park boundaries, was one of the sources of supplementary income for residents, but closed in 1920. Cabin Branch marketed sulphuric acid, a derivative of pyrite or "fool's gold." The output was transported from the mine to the Potomac on a narrow gauge railroad nicknamed "The Dinky" by area residents. Engineer John Kendall piloted the train down through Dumfries, along the route of present-day Mine Road to Possum Point, where the Barrow Company had a landing facility. It was because of an impending strike that the owner closed the mine in 1920. The company said it could not afford to pay the miners more than fifty cents a day and meet the competition from higher grade sulphuric acid then on the market. As part of the public programs, rangers lead hikes to the mine site.[7]
Courtesy of the Prince William Forest Park

Foundations of an old school can be seen by hikers who follow Trail No. 7. This is one of seven school sites known to park service historians.
Courtesy of the Prince William Forest Park

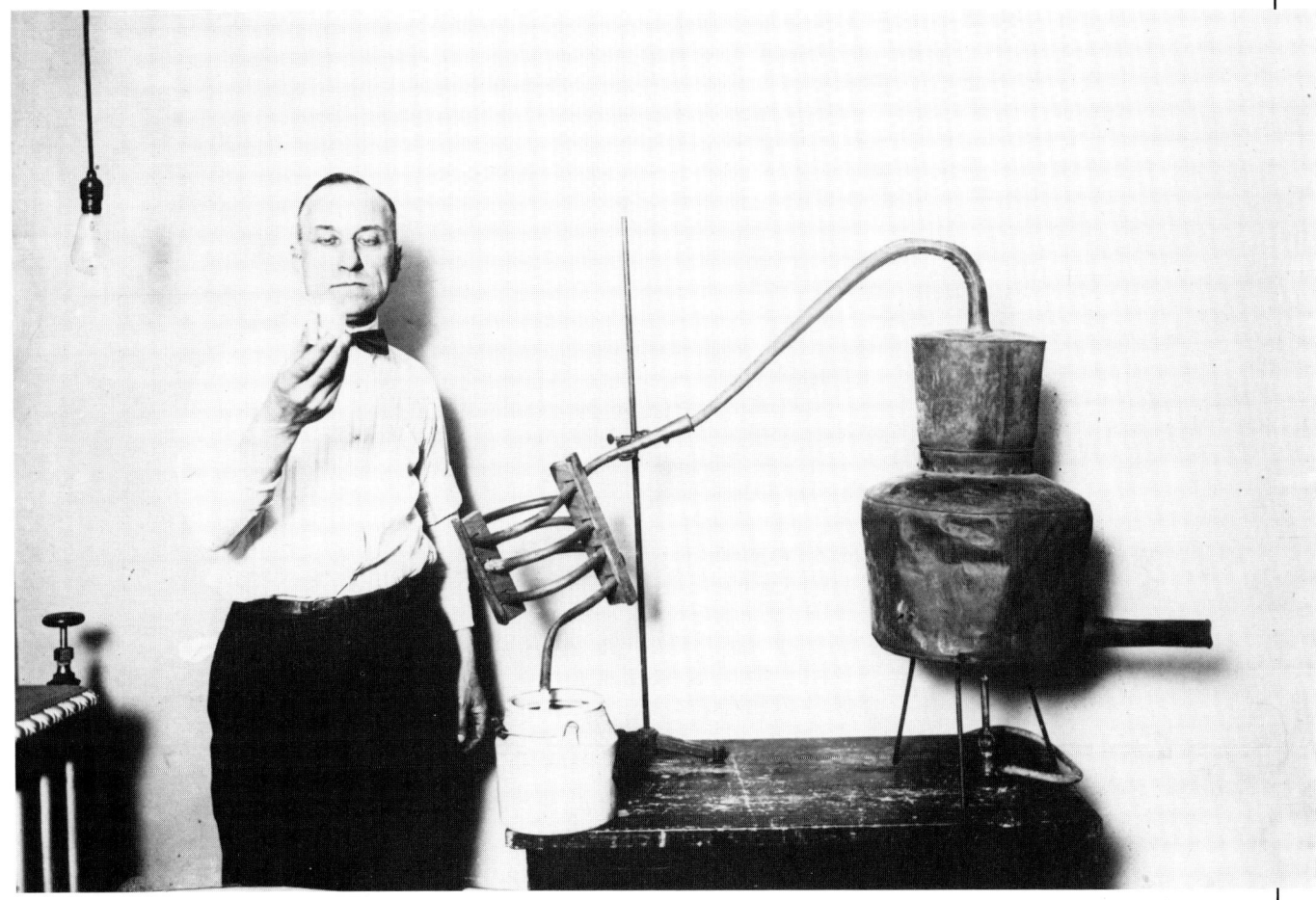

One supplementary means of making money, reportedly more prevalent in the secluded woodlands of Chopawamsic RDA than most other places, was the operation of stills to make illegal liquor. The severity of the Depression experienced there made the temptation even greater, although the poor generally did not have the money to buy the sugar needed to make a lot of whiskey. The maxim that it takes money to make money was true even in making moonshine.

An unlawful operation could be spotted by the revenue officer by the smoke from the fire, lit near a little run, far from any houses. Hunters wandering through the woods might come upon a still unexpectedly. If they said nothing and kept going, no harm would come to them. To interfere with a bootlegger, however, was to encounter real danger.

The law officer's daughter who remembers the bullet hole in the family car after her father helped raid a still; the politician who remembers being told by a local leader, "I will support you, but stay out of my district," and the Hickory Ridge resident who remembers a neighbor badly beaten, because his moonshine sales were cutting into the business of a competitor—these are witnesses to the cancer of lawlessness that corrodes the character of a community when it treats illegal activity as a joke, or, more tellingly, supports it by buying the product. Contrary to popular supposition, making whiskey illegally, i.e., without meeting government standards for commercial marketing and paying a tax on the product, is not an enterprise exclusive to the Prohibition years.

The court house records of Prince William County indicate there was always a supply of homemade stills like the one in the picture being used in evidence and then destroyed. More stills would be constructed to take their place. In only two instances is there a record that the moonshiners met their match. They lost a round to Marine Gen. Smedley Butler, who said their product was poisoning his men, and who exerted economic pressure to clear the town of Quantico. Finally, during World War II, bootleggers found the forestland of Chopawamsic RDA inhabited by a species even rougher and more territorial than they were—the agents of the Office of Special Services.
Courtesy of the Library of Congress

The winter of 1939 to 1940 brought heavy snow. The photographer titled this picture of his fellow Civilian Conservation Corps trainees The Mad Russian and His Snow Detail, *proving young men in any generation are prone to high jinks with their hard work.*
Courtesy of the Prince William Forest Park

TRANSITION TIME

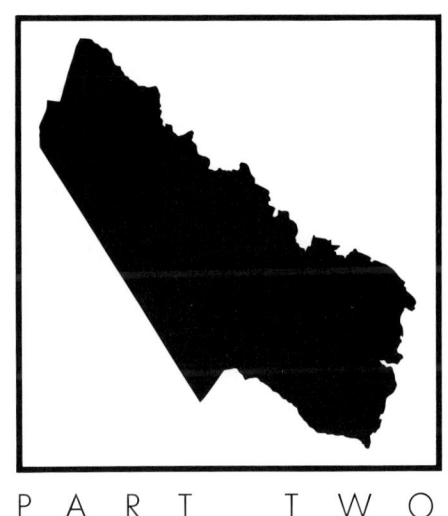

PART TWO

Chopawamsic Recreation Demonstration Project or Area was not officially christened by Act of Congress until August 13, 1940. Civilian Conservation Corps (CCC) worker George Bezuko snapped this photo of his friend Alagrucci in front of the original park entrance sometime between 1939 and 1941. By the donation of the pictures he took while at a CCC camp near Joplin from 1939 until 1941, George Bezuko has given us a look at representatives of a generation which came of age when one of four men could not find employment.
Courtesy of the Prince William Forest Park

"Unpowered road-grader" (according to the label), the CCC also had the use of a motorized grader, but they had not finished the roads connecting all the cabin camps when World War II brought construction to a halt.
Courtesy of the Prince William Forest Park

Hitchhiking in Triangle was a much safer and more acceptable procedure in those pre-war days, although Triangle was less of a metropolis than it is now.
Courtesy of the Prince William Forest Park

113

Sightseeing in the nation's capital, was always of interest to those nearby.
Courtesy of the Prince William Forest Park

The first cabin camp was scheduled to open in the summer of 1937, but that winter one of the CCC companies building the RDA was taken off the job and sent elsewhere. It looked as though the first group of children would have to wait a year. After consultation, the park management and the social service agencies decided instead to make do with the incomplete facilities and to have the campers themselves help with the work still to be done. Shown here, in the summer of 1937, campers are in the water where a crib dam eventually will create a swimming area.
Courtesy of the Prince William Forest Park

Boys and girls take advantage of the out-of-doors for storytime and pitching horseshoes. Courtesy of the Prince William Forest Park

This CCC camp served as the Area A headquarters and basic school for OSS personnel. It was built for year-round occupation, which the cabin camps were not. Students in the latter were reportedly unhappy with their lot as fall progressed into the winter of 1942. Ultimately the OSS winterized the cabin camps it used, an advantageous result of its occupation. Courtesy of the National Archives

Wartime In The Forest

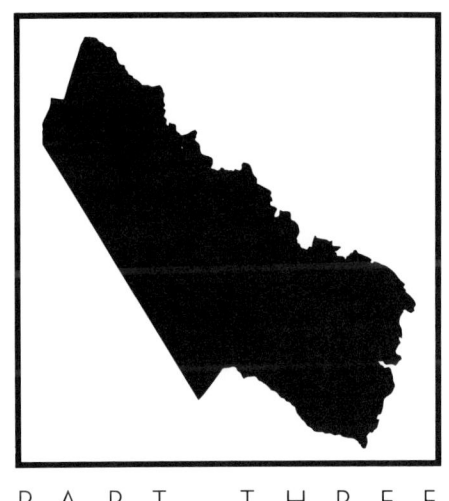

PART THREE

The school and training staff of the Office of Special Services, which operated a number of schools in the Washington area is shown here. American students came from all the armed services, both officers and enlisted, male and female. There were not many women, but the students accepted were excellent material, so wrote a reporting officer. There were also civilian agent trainees, and occasionally foreign recruits, who were trained and sent back to their respective countries.
Courtesy of the National Archives

Gen. William J. Donovan, director of the Office of Special Services, World War II predecessor of the Central Intelligence Agency (CIA), once said guerrilla warfare is designed to do more than kill and destroy. It is meant to generate an atmosphere of fear and insecurity, to keep the enemy "looking over his shoulder."[1] Less than a century before Donovan enunciated this goal, Col. John Singleton Mosby practiced the principle as he and his guerrilla band probed for weak spots in the Union supply lines along the lonely roads of eastern Prince William. Colonel Mosby would have made a very effective instructor in the classes that were held in those same woods during World War II.

From 1942 to 1945 Chopawamsic RDA became the cryptic Area A and adjacent Area C, used by the Office of Special Services (OSS), to train secret agents. The OSS was the predecessor of the present CIA. It was begun by an agreement between President Roosevelt and a prominent lawyer named William Donovan, just before Pearl Harbor. The president felt the need to have more intelligence available than he then had. Donovan, he had been told, was the best qualified person to put together such an operation. After the Japanese attack on Hawaii, the start-up of the new agency went into high gear. By June 1942, four training schools were operational. Two of them, Chopawamsic and its sister RDA in the Catoctin Mountains of Maryland, were logical choices for the Schools and Training Branch of OSS. Both were large, secluded federal premises, within easy driving distance of the capital. They were not ideal, so wrote the reporting army colonel in 1943, but they were the best available at that time. The self-contained campsites, designed to make it possible for different organizations to camp at the same time, also facilitated outdoor studies of a deadlier nature.[2]

The OSS staff ran both basic and advanced training at the same time in different sections of Chopawamsic, which was known as Area A. A former CCC camp (there had been three in the park) served as both headquarters and the A-4 area was used for basic classes. Among the studies required at the entry level were map reading, use of pistols, revolvers, and rifles, code, first aid, malaria control, chemical warfare, and demolition and explosives.

The demolition class was a useful one as seen by the postwar administrators, because it got the unwanted

118

These men are part of a class in Morse code techniques of the OSS, generated in Area C, adjacent to the park. The training at this school was in communications. Most of the trainees already knew Morse code when they arrived.
Courtesy of the National Archives

buildings on the former small holdings out of the way—with only one oversight. One class blew up a house which the government had considered buying. It had been appraised, but had not yet been purchased. Fortunately, the owner was in Philadelphia, not living in the house, and the Army Engineers recouped the situation by completing the purchase at the appraised value.[3]

The advanced class, held in a cabin camp designated A-3, included subversive warfare, lock picking, cover, control of civilian population, and close combat and knife fighting. Most military officers began at this level, having already had most of the basics. Two other cabin units, designated A-2 and A-5, were used for incoming and outgoing students.[4]

One of the peripheral hazards of the course was that axis agents would try to infiltrate the OSS. Superintendent Lykes of the National Park Service was present on one occasion when the OSS staff thought this had been done. He was handed a gun and told to join the search for a missing student. If he should see the student, he was told, "Shoot first and ask questions afterward." Lykes was thankful he did not find the missing person.[5]

Once trained, the secret agents received assignments to North Africa, the Middle East, the Far East, Europe, and the Pacific. Their new identities required documentation. Even such mundane actions as buying new footwear presented a logistical problem in wartime, when civilians had to have ration stamps to buy shoes.
Courtesy of the National Archives

Photograph by Abbie Rowe, courtesy of the Prince William Forest Park

AFTER THE WAR

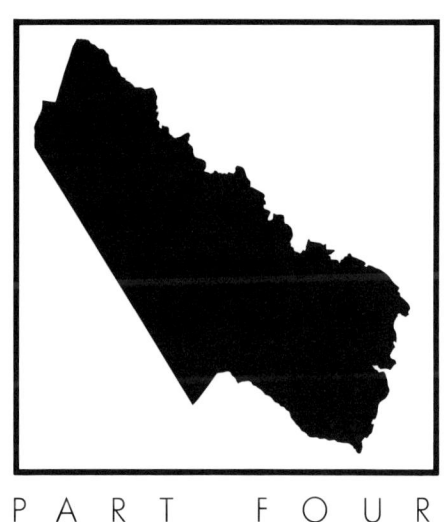

PART FOUR

Americans of all ages still enjoyed the out-of-doors, but note the tendency in these outings of the 1950s to treat the forest as backyard fun and the clothing of pre-jeans age.

Photograph by Abbie Rowe, courtesy of the Prince William Forest Park

Courtesy of the Prince William Forest Park

In 1945 the war was over. The guard dogs and the saboteur trainees departed, and Capt. Ira B. Lykes, USMC, stopped going next door to Quantico to work and became Superintendent Lykes of the National Park Service again.

Several other changes came about at the war's end or near it. The name was officially changed from Chopawamsic RDA to Prince William Forest Park in August 1948, and the connecting roads between campsites were built by the Army Engineers from Fort Belvoir as part of their practice exercises, a matter that resulted in considerable saving to the Park Service.[1]

Meanwhile, the campers returned and life in the forest was again as it had been intended, but not without problems. In supervising and observing the operations of the five cabin camps, Lykes found a notable lack of knowledge concerning their natural surroundings among the camp staff as well as among the campers. The campers wanted to learn about nature, he wrote, but as the counselors knew little about the subject themselves, they taught what they did know such as athletic skills or crafts, which could have been taught just as well in the city. Like Lord Baden Powell in South Africa, Lykes found that a generation of city dwellers had lost the ability to be at home in natural surroundings.[2]

As time went on, campers in the 1950s did more fully utilize the forest setting. Photograph by Abbie Rowe, courtesy of the Prince William Forest Park

Courtesy of the Prince William Forest Park

Courtesy of the Prince William Forest Park

Sometimes they chose activities that conjured up the Indian inhabitants of a bygone era. The Jewish Community Center favored reenactment, while the Girl Scouts crafted a name for their unit, Camp Mawavi, to reflect input from (Ma)ryland, (Wa)shington and (Vi)rginia, because it sounded like an Indian word.[3]

The planners added campout sites for the whole family. Many enjoyed this opportunity for back to nature weekends. Courtesy of the Prince William Forest Park

Photograph by David Vassar, courtesy of the Prince William Forest Park

The Park rangers themselves filled in the gaps for teachers, by being available, by leading walks, and by putting up signs for self-guided hikes. Those not familiar with the ways of the beaver, might not recognize its handiwork.
Courtesy of the Prince William Forest Park

Tourist business brought in by the new federal highway and employment offered by the Marine base next door to them were an economic tonic for Dumfries. The eighteenth-century Stagecoach Inn had been renovated and porches added to suit the twentieth century.
Courtesy of the National Archives

CHAPTER 8
PRINCE WILLIAM FACES THE FUTURE

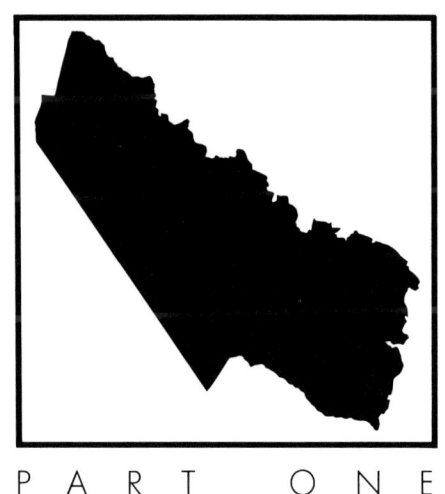

PART ONE

Approaching Dumfries from the south on the unpaved Potomac Path, about 1910, you would have seen more horse-drawn conveyances like the one ahead than cars.

*B. Keys' cornfield is on the left, a cemetery out of the picture is on the right.
Courtesy of the Weems-Botts Museum, Cecil Garrison collection*

Even at the beginning of the century, when America's population lived mainly in rural areas, the Bureau of the Census reserved a separate category for rural counties near large towns or cities. The population that has access to the facilities of a city does not suffer the same limitations nor isolation as completely rural areas.

Whatever else it had done, this advantage of being near the city of Washington had not resulted in growth for Prince William. At the beginning of the twentieth century its population of just over eleven thousand was almost exactly the same as it had been at the end of the Revolution. Half a century later in 1950, however, the population had almost doubled, reading just over twenty-one thousand.

The years immediately after World War II were the watershed years for the Washington metropolitan area. As the federal government expanded, many companies established research and development, and lobbying offices in the area. Within forty years more than 2.5 million people became new residents.[1]

Beginning in 1946, many of these newcomers were returning veterans with young growing families. Existing housing could not accommodate them all. New suburbs developed primarily along the transportation access routes, tracks on which the newcomers rolled from home to work and back. The developments spread outward like the tide reaching Prince William in the 1950s, as Interstate 95 unrolled southward from the Occoquan to the Chopawamsic.

The buildup began gradually years before. Even before World War II, the new role the federal government assumed in highway building helped change the face of the towns by the 1930s. Some of the first signs of growth were, logically and appropriately, where Prince William County got its urban start, near Dumfries. The following pictures give a taste of the contrasts that developed as the motor age progressed.

Still heading north, the Potomac Path becomes Main Street in Dumfries, where one of the new horseless carriages is in view. Beginning in the lower left corner, the houses belong to: Johnnie Brawner, Charles Brawner, a blacksmith's shop, Charles McInter (?), Ella Waters, and Cosmo Gallahand. Beginning at the lower right corner, the owners were: Clay Speakes, Dellie Crawford, George Ratcliffe, the Odd Fellows Hall, and Robert King. Courtesy of the Weems-Botts Museum, Cecil Garrison collection

Should you have needed to buy anything or mail a letter, you could stop at Garrison's store, which also housed the post office. The lack of signs announcing the store's name or town post office was typical and lamented by early motorists, who were often lost and in need of directions even when no one was available to give them. Courtesy of the Weems-Botts Museum, Cecil Garrison collection

Garrison lived next to his store, a convenient arrangement and a common one. Courtesy of the Weems-Botts Museum, Cecil Garrison collection

*Looking toward Main Street from Washington Street, it appears that many of the residents had mini-farms inside the town limits: plowed areas for gardens and barns for storage and stock raising. The steeple on the right in the distance belongs to the Baptist Church with Bailey's Hill beyond it.
Courtesy of the Weems-Botts Museum, Cecil Garrison collection*

As the notations on these old pictures show, Dumfries residents were proud of their antecedents even then. Williams Ordinary, the Old Dumfries Hotel (circa 1790) was still in use, but Tebbs house (circa 1749), once the town showplace, was unoccupied and considered haunted.
Courtesy of the Weems-Botts Museum, Cecil Garrison collection

Another landmark was this old mill, circa 1800, which did not continue operating as long as many in the county. These eight photos were donated to the Weems-Botts Museum collection by Cecil Garrison and annotated by him.
Courtesy of the Weems-Botts Museum, Cecil Garrison collection

The Episcopal Church in Dumfries Cemetery was the third in the colonial parish. The first had so deteriorated by 1752, it was sold and replaced by a new brick building. What happened to these has not been determined. This picture is the property of Goldie Keys Brawner, who was christened in the church and attended services there with her family. Afterward the circuit riding minister often had dinner at the Keys farm. The church burned one night about 1924. It had ceased to be an active church and moonshiners were making illegal whiskey there when their still exploded. Cecil Garrison, who lived nearby, ran out when he heard the explosion, and claimed to have recognized the men running from the church.[2]
Courtesy of the Weems-Botts Museum, Cecil Garrison collection

By the time a Marine aviator took this picture in 1931, the Potomac Path had been paved and renamed U.S. Highway 1. The house on the left belonged to Guy Cline and had been built from a kit ordered from Sears, Roebuck and Company. It has been tentatively identified as No. 183, a model available in 1912, 1913, and 1916 Sears catalogs. Cline's friend, Sam Bauckman, liked the finished product so much, he copied it. Both houses, in beautiful repair, are still standing.[3]
Courtesy of the Weems-Botts Museum

Just outside the range of the camera in the previous picture, was the Quantico Creek Garage, owned and operated in the 1930s by John W. and Mamie V. Clarke. In the early 1940s the building was converted to a private home and rental units. It burned down about 1945 and is presently the site of Henderson Village.
Courtesy of the Weems-Botts Museum

If the river marshes were popular with duck hunters, there was sport inland hunting rabbits. These friends hunted together in 1915, when the picture was taken, and for years afterward. They are, left to right: Randolph Brawner, Cecil Garrison, and Kloman Wheat. Courtesy of the Weems-Botts Museum

Not far from Dumfries stood the old Ewell house where Parson Weems had also lived. Intrigued by its history, George C. Round had bought and restored the house in the late nineteenth century and had even written a romantic account of one of its first occupants, Miriamne Ewell, who married Dr. James Craik. Round never managed to convince his wife she would be happy spending summers there, so he eventually sold Bel Air. By 1936, when this picture was taken, the house was vacant and for sale again.[4] Though Bel Air had been empty for eighteen years in 1948 when Dr. and Mrs. W. E. S. Flory bought it, there were still many interior details to recommend the house. All the window replacements had to be custom made, so storm windows were the interim solution. The Florys bought Bel Air in September 1948 and moved in the following April. Courtesy of the Library of Congress

Dr. Flory found getting a good picture of his new property difficult, because of the undergrowth. It took the ministrations of several goats to mow the savannah.
Courtesy of Dr. W. E. S. Flory

The success of their restoration of Bel Air and the interest in historic preservation generated by it encouraged Anne Flory to continue in the field. She became chairman of the Prince William County Historical Commission, and she spearheaded the effort to save the Parson Weems office building in Dumfries from demolition and replacement with office buildings.
Courtesy of Dr. W. E. S. Flory

This is the Weems-Botts House as it appeared in 1949. Since just after the Civil War, it had been used as a residence by the Merchant family, whose members first came to Dumfries in the eighteenth century.
Drawing by Lee Lansing, courtesy of the Weems-Botts Museum

The last to live in the old house were Annie Merchant and her daughter, Violet. The latter died in 1968 at the age of eighty-two. It was not until six years later, in 1974, that the Town of Dumfries purchased the house. It was restored and is now operated as a museum.
Courtesy of the Weems-Botts Museum

No sooner had the town discovered in 1961, that it still had incorporated status due to its charters granted in 1749 and 1872, than it elected a mayor and council for the first time in many years. It was with a subsequent election, however, that Dumfries drew international attention to itself. One of the new council members in 1963 was a proprietor of an auto repair business, a native of the Dumfries area, and a respected citizen of the town. What was unusual about Wilmer Portner, from the perspective of Virginia history, was that he was the first black man elected to municipal office in the Old Dominion since Reconstruction, the years immediately after the Civil War. At a time when other sections of the state were drawing unfavorable notice by their refusal to desegregate the schools, Dumfries' action was a reprieve for the U.S. Information Agency (U.S.I.A.) which likes to point with pride. Attendees at the meeting featured in a U.S.I.A. story were, clockwise left to right: George Waters, Ed Fraley, Reuel Waters (George's brother), Wilmer Porter, Randolph Brawner, Guy Reynolds, Nick Katsarelis, and Cecil Garrison.
Courtesy of Wilmer Porter

Not long after Wilmer Porter began serving on the Dumfries Town Council, his wife Mary was chosen as one of four black teachers to begin the pilot desegregation program in Prince William County. A native of Farmville, Virginia, with a college degree in education, Mary Porter began her teaching career in Prince William just before World War II. Her first assignment was in the three-room Cabin Branch School near the mine. For the pilot year, she was assigned to Dumfries Elementary, only a short walk from her home, where she spent the subsequent sixteen years before retirement. The transition year presented no serious problems, she said, adding that she felt this was partly due to the influence of the Marine families, whose years of travel had given them a broader than average perspective.
Courtesy of Wilmer and Mary Porter

The Porters were feted at a dinner at the American Legion Hall in Dumfries after his retirement in 1980. Seated with the Porters at the head table were their two daughters, both teachers, and their husbands, left to right: Hazel and Ronald Scites, Mary and Wilmer Porter, and Gwendolyn and Clyde Washington.
Courtesy of Wilmer and Mary Porter

At his retirement in 1980, Wilmer Porter posed with the mayors with whom he had served in his years on the council. Left to right: Willard Mountjoy, Martha Black, J. K. Garrison, Porter, Paul Cleary, Ed Fraley, and Alton Mountjoy.
Courtesy of Wilmer and Mary Porter

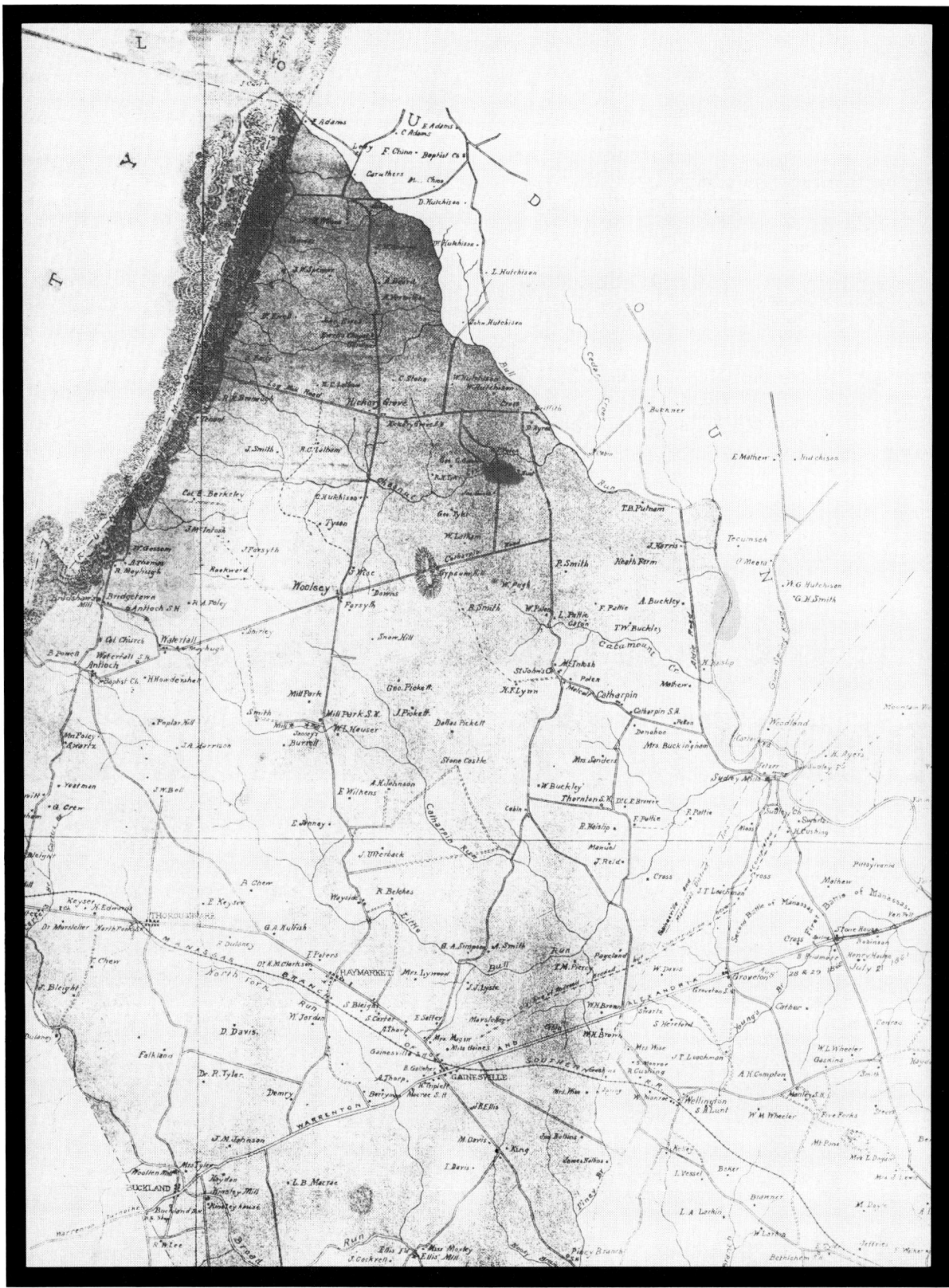

1901 map by William H. Brown, Gainesville, Virginia

HOW THE CITY REACHED PRINCE WILLIAM

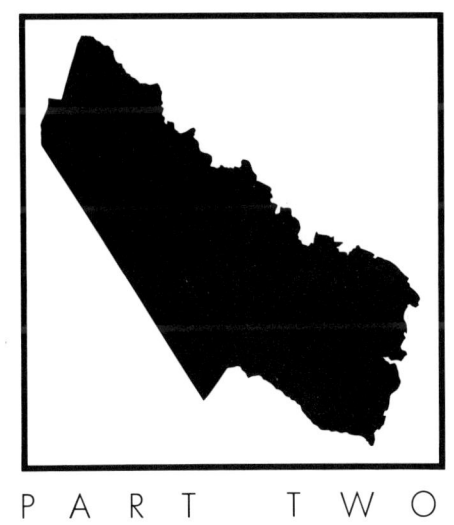

PART TWO

As Dumfries came of age in modern times, there were gradual changes in other parts of the county as well.

Wavery lies in ruins, this once imposing mansion with its unusual rounded dormers and view of the Bull Run mountains. Built at great expense in 1836, it burned in 1973. Its most famous owner, Eli H. Janney, a Loudoun County native, invented the automatic coupling device for railroad cars and bought the plantation in the late nineteenth century. Shown here at the time the picture of the Haymarket Agricultural Club was taken, Waverly was owned by Colonel DePauw, a brother of the founder of DePauw University.
Photographs courtesy of Marianna Durst

The group of men in this 1905 picture of the Haymarket Agricultural Club taken at Waverly still included representatives of the prewar landowning families, such as Col. Ed Berkeley of Evergreen. Back row, left to right: Col. Newland DePauw, Waverly Farm; Louis Henson, Burnside; Christian Heineken, Mill Park; William Dodge, Bonnie Brae; Franz Peters, Batavia; William Brown; and Edmund Wilkins, a guest. Front row: unknown, Dr. Clarkson, Wateree; Colonel Berkeley, Evergreen; Andrew Lowe; and Bowman Price.
Courtesy of Manassas City Museum

This is Evergreen as it was in 1936. The house was built by Lewis Berkeley in 1827. The 1,000-acre plantation came to the Berkeleys through marriage alliance with the Carters. In 1940 the 660-acre estate was modernized by new owners, and in 1968 another set of owners sold Evergreen to a group of Manassas businessmen. They converted 225 acres into a golf course, and have been selling the rest in 3 to 12-acre lots. Plans to use the old home as a clubhouse did not materialize. Older houses, such as Evergreen, often require more structural alteration for adaptive use than is practicable.[1]
Courtesy of the Library of Congress

Effingham, built about 1765 by a member of the Alexander family from whom the town took its name, is one of the few examples remaining of the complex of buildings around the great house of a self-sufficient plantation. As the home of a prominent doctor in the 1960s, it was the scene of much social activity.[2]
Courtesy of the Library of Congress

One of the most noticeable changes in western Prince William was the shrinking number of dairy farms. In 1956 there were still ninety-one dairy farms in Prince William County. In 1968, there were only thirty-two, but their production was proportionately higher.³ Many of the farmers had sold their farms to developers and retired. Few were as innovative as "Granny" Hersch, shown here at the gate of what she and her husband called the Fun Farm. Born Mabel Harley, she and her husband, Orville Hersch, decided to "have fun with their farm," when they reached retirement age and found none of their children wanted to follow in their footsteps. Rather than sell the farm, they sold the cows and conducted excursions around their land for city children: Scout troops, school classes, and private parties. The Herschs did not charge for their tours, but donations the visitors cared to give were sent to farm organizations to help Third World countries. Ten dollars, for example, would give a farm family in an undeveloped country a starter flock of chicks.⁴
Courtesy of the Manassas City Museum

One of the most difficult properties to develop in the west of Prince William County is called the "Williams Tract." Its strategic importance, on the corner of two arterial highways, can be seen in this picture. Its historical importance lies in its position adjacent to the Manassas National Battlefield Park. Two efforts at commercial development have failed: one was a proposal by the Marriott Corporation to build a theme amusement park of a Disneyland type. Most recently a developer proposed a regional shopping and office complex and aroused local residents to the extent they persuaded Congress to buy the property for the National Park Service.
Courtesy of the Prince William County Office of Economic Development

In the eastern end of the County, development has followed a somewhat different pattern. Although the Richmond, Fredericksburg and Potomac Railroad (RF&P) had built the final land-link to Washington after the Civil War, this did not stimulate development in eastern Prince William as much as the Orange and Alexandria Railroad, later the Southern Railroad, did in the west. Perhaps it was because the railroad skipped like a stone skimmed across the water over the peninsulas that had been colonial plantations. Little commercial development had taken place there after the tobacco bubble burst. This was a fortunate circumstance for the ecology. It made the wetlands along the river accessible to wealthy sportsmen, who could afford to buy the land and merely hold it in a natural state.
Courtesy of the Prince William County Office of Economic Development

These cottages on Possum Point were owned by wealthy District of Columbia sportsmen. The railroad from the pyrite mine came through this area also. Both the narrow guage railroad and the hunt club were being removed when these photographs were taken in 1948 to make way for a Virginia Electric and Power Company power station.
Courtesy of Virginia Power and the Weems-Botts Museum

This is the remains of the boathouse at the Possum Point Hunt Club.
Courtesy of Virginia Power and the Weems-Botts Museum

The caretaker at the Possum Point Hunting Lodge was a Mr. Emory who also ran a small farm seen in this picture.[4]
Courtesy of Virginia Power and the Weems-Botts Museum

The construction of the Possum Point Power Station necessitated some alterations along the tracks of the RF&P observed in this picture. At another hunt club up the river on the old Leesylvania site, visitors from New York were said to arrive on the RF&P in their private cars at the turn of the century. The cars were put off on a siding, and the visitors could choose whether to stay in the cars or bunk at the lodge up the hill.
Courtesy of Virginia Power and the Weems-Botts Museum

The hunt club on what was formerly Leesylvania was called Freestone after the rocky point. The rock was considered free from faults and good for building. Butch Hampton, who grew up on Freestone Point in the 1930s, played frequently with his dog. There were no other children at the end of the dirt road that led to the hunt club. Butch's father, William A. "Doc" Hampton was the manager. Among his other chores, Doc kept the duck blinds in repair. The blinds were little cubicles on stilts built in the marshlands, easily damaged by ice or bad weather. Hampton sometimes hired people to help him if there were a large party of hunters. The blinds had to be made ready, the guns loaded and put out, and the ducks retrieved after they were shot.

Butch remembers the hunt club owner's wife, Mrs. Wheelock, a friendly lady who came with her husband sometimes in the off-season. If Butch's mother wasn't looking, he would go up to see Mrs. Wheelock at the lodge on the hill. There, he remembers, was the "little red wagon," a liquor laden bar that came out of a concealed door in the wall when an overhead bell was rung, and a building behind the club that contained about ten lead-lined ice boxes to store the ducks after they were shot.
Courtesy of William A. Hampton, Jr.

The earliest phase of hunt club history Butch Hampton remembers began in 1926 when William Wheelock and Percy Chubb jointly leased the hunting property on Neabsco and Powells creeks.
Courtesy of J. H. Joynt

To see whether duck hunting at Freestone was as good as reported, the lessees kept careful count. As W. H. Wheelock noted, he and Percy Chubb did decide to buy Freestone Point and enjoyed over a decade of hunting on the former colonial grant.
Courtesy of J. H. Joynt

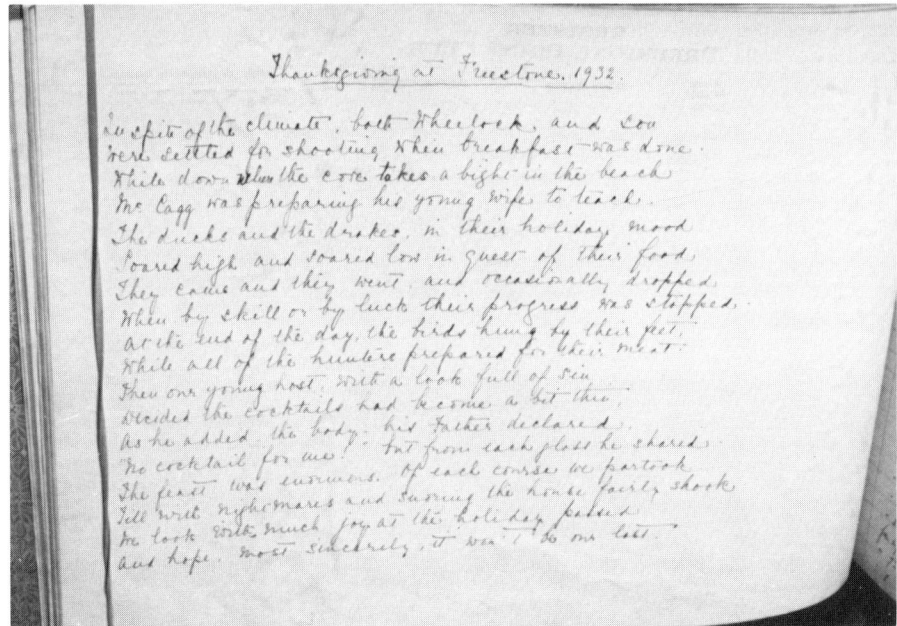

The Wheelocks appear to have had an inclination to write about their good times at Freestone on the backs of the register pages.
Courtesy of J. H. Joynt

The Freestone lodge owners may have been more willing to share their new pastime with their wives than the latter were to join them in the duck blinds in the cold light of dawn.
Courtesy of J. H. Joynt

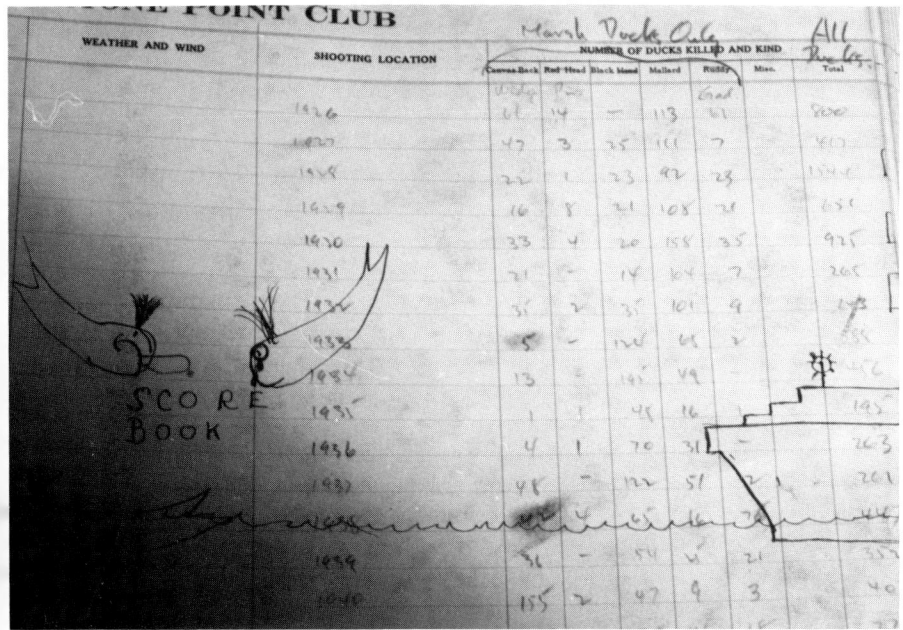

The overall statistics kept in the register indicate a steady decline in the number of ducks shot, from 1,544 in 1928 to 272 in 1941. In 1942 the Freestone Point Club became the property of a prominent Alexandria attorney, J. Howard Joynt. Joynt often brought his family to Freestone as had the New York owners. Martha Joynt Kumar believes she or her brother were responsible for the art work on the title page of the register. The young people did not entirely approve of their parent's new hobby, although they liked the surroundings very much.
Courtesy of J. H. Joynt

J. Howard Joynt is shown here in 1949 in the former lodge, which he had extensively renovated. He was told the property was put up for sale because the New Yorker most interested in continued hunting, Morgan Wheelock, a son of one of the owners, had gone into the service for the duration of World War II.[5]
Courtesy of J. H. Joynt

Two friends of Joynt's, Frank Kinnard (left) and Thomas Hulfish, also Alexandrians, were with him at Freestone in December 1949 when this picture was taken. It was Hulfish who had introduced the new owner to duck hunting the year before the property was purchased and then urged him to buy Freestone when it came on the market.
Courtesy of J. H. Joynt

Joining Messrs. Joynt and Kinnard in this photo, also taken in 1947, are (left) Doc Hampton and (far right) Tom Hulfish's father.
Courtesy of J. H. Joynt

The three friends are shown here in front of the lodge in 1947 after a day of successful shooting. Left to right, Hulfish, Joynt and Kinnard.
Courtesy of J. H. Joynt

This was the Freestone property manager's house at the foot of the hill below the lodge, where the Hamptons lived.
Courtesy of J. H. Joynt

Besides his job as a hunt club manager, Doc Hampton was a commercial fisherman, one of the first to catch and market eels, which had to be shipped abroad. In this picture he was giving his daughters, Barbara and Delores, and his sister-in-law, Leighanna Gay, a ride in his new 1949 pickup. Most of the time, however, Hampton stacked the truck with catfish, perch, and rockfish on blocks of ice, covered with a tarpaulin, and drove to Baltimore to sell them. Other commercial fishermen sold their catch to the "buy boats" which cruised the Potomac collecting wares for the Washington market.[6]
Courtesy of W. A. Hampton, Jr.

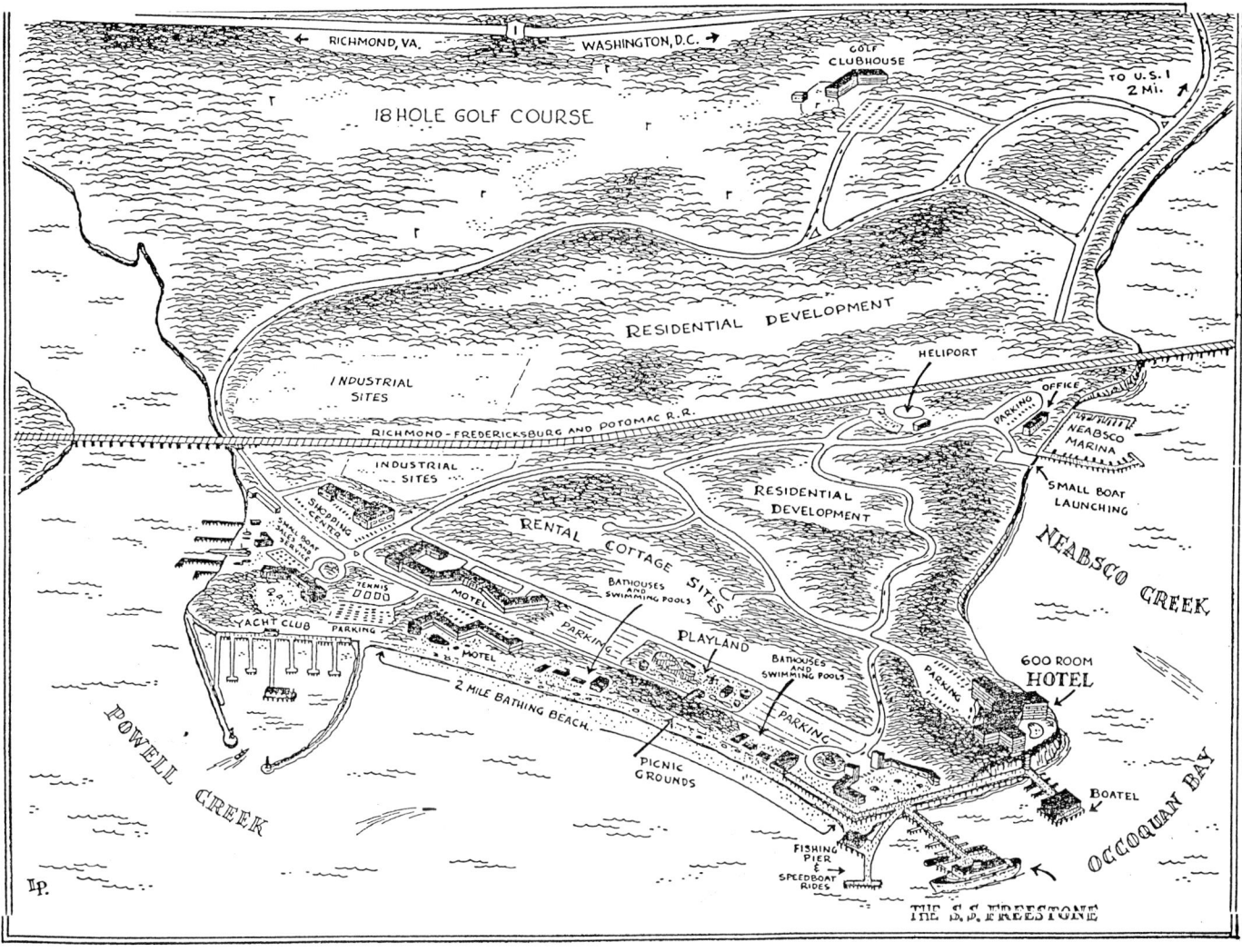

The river pollution and the development of residential housing along the river eventually drove the fowl of the Atlantic Flyway to the Eastern Shore. These circumstances also diminished Freestone's value as a hunting property. Joynt sold Freestone and bought another fishing property in Dorchester County, Maryland. In July 1957, however, another enterprise began. As the promotion poster demonstrates, developer J. Carl Hill of Arlington had plans for the type of diversification prevalent in the 1980s. The only parts of the drawing which materialized in this case were (at the lower right of the picture) the swimming pool, beach, parking lot, and the presence of the S.S. *Freestone*.
Courtesy of the Leesylvania State Park

The excursion ship Tolchester, *rechristened the S.S.* Freestone, *was only moored at the pier adjacent to Freestone Point from 1957 to 1958. It was technically in Maryland, since the boundary was fixed in colonial times at the highwater mark on the Virginia shore. Both the liquor in this bar and the 175 slot machines on the S.S.* Freestone *were illegal in Virginia. Despite a heavy weekend trade, there was strong protest from both state governors, and the Maryland gambling license was revoked. The ship was forced to close in 1958 in the face of suits for a collective debt of eighty-eight thousand dollars.*
Courtesy of Mrs. William W. White, Jr.

Billy White and his unidentified friend do not have a lot of company at the Freestone Point swimming pool. Billy's father, William Wesley White, was the manager of the complex at the time the gambling ship was there and tried to make the park pay as a family recreation center after the ship was taken away.[7]
Courtesy of Mrs. William W. White, Jr.

Although Bill White's efforts to keep the Freestone Point Park afloat were not successful in 1960, he was looking for customers on the most populated side of the county. The earliest Hylton subdivision, Marumsco Village, was built near Woodbridge and the growth beginning at the northern boundary is evident on this 1963 map.

The wild natural beauty of Freestone Point was saved for everyone to enjoy in 1978 by a donation and a matching grant. The donation was in the form of an offer by owner Daniel K. Ludwig to sell the 505 acres for half their appraised value of four million dollars. The matching grant was obtained by the state of Virginia from the federal government. The most active architects of the measure were Don Curtis, the Prince William Historical Commission chairman in 1978, and Eleanor Lee Templeman, a descendent of the Lees of Leesylvania. Curtis is a descendent of a family which has lived in the vicinity of Leesylvania State Park since 1701, so it would be fair to call his action neighborly. The park is expected to open in 1989 or 1990.[8]

Courtesy of Mrs. Wm. W. White, Jr.

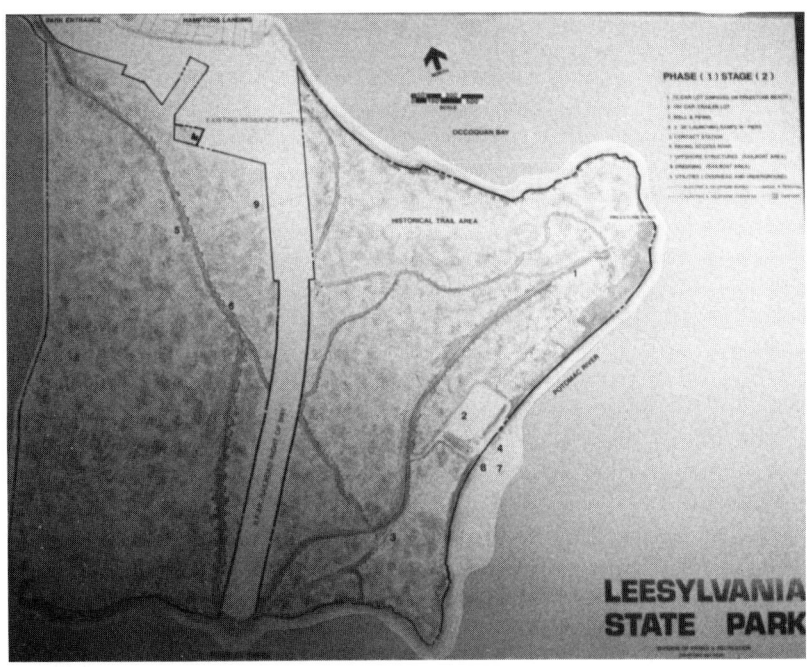

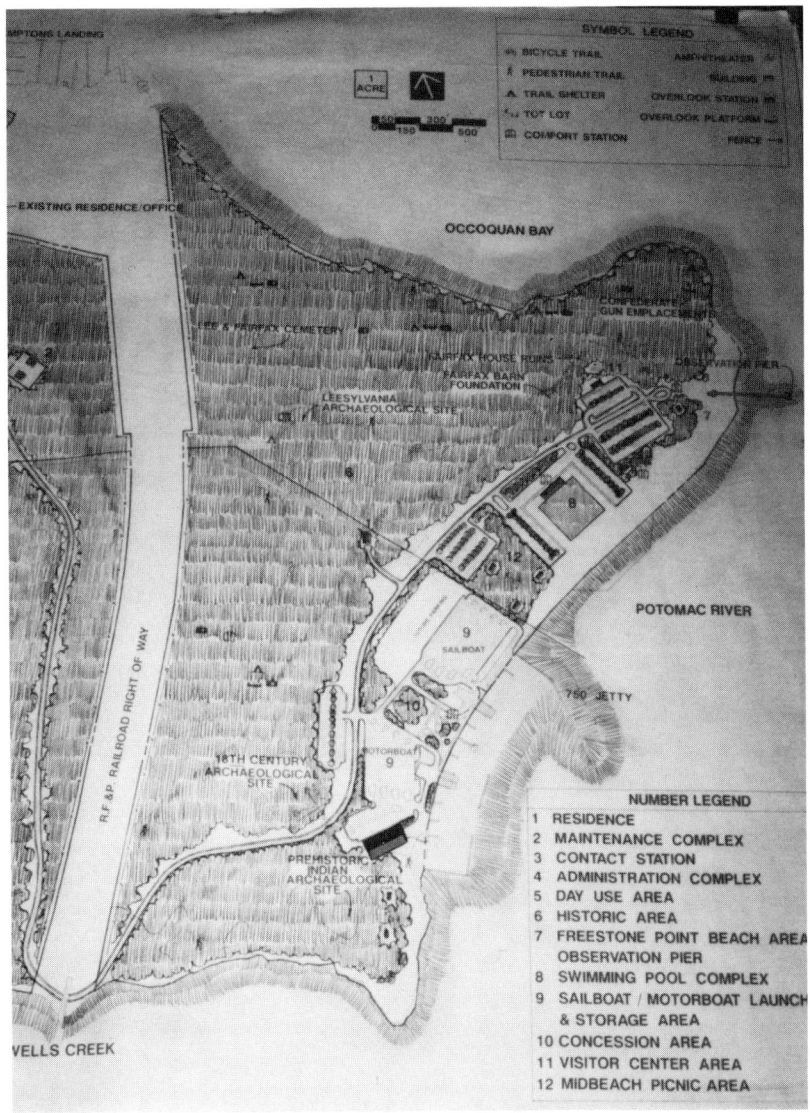

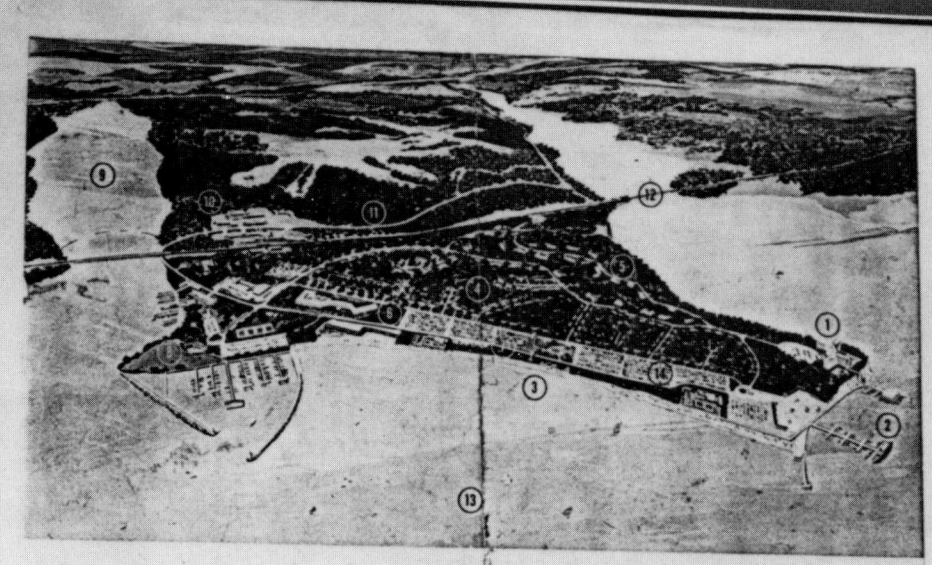

In this May 20, 1937 aerial view of Leesylvania, the hunting lodge is visible at the top of the hill. Near the water the lighter shade indicates second growth forest where there were plantation tobacco fields.
Map courtesy of the Leesylvania State Park

The State park in 1988 has a different access route.
Map courtesy of the Leesylvania State Park

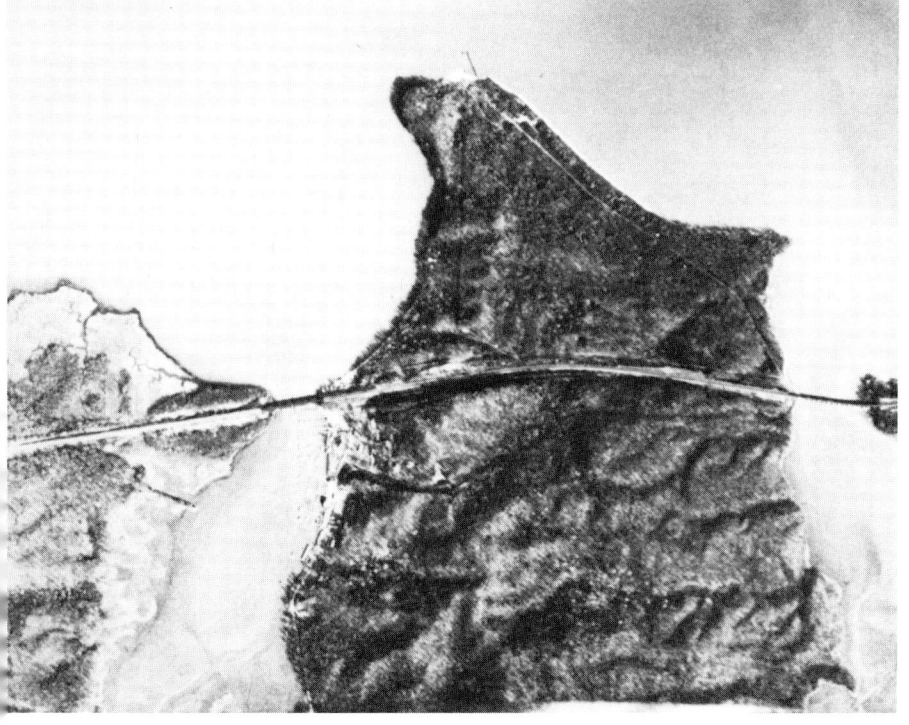

Down river the Possum Point Power Station covers the ground once occupied by "the dinky" railroad, the landing, and the hunt club. The plant has grown since its beginning in 1948 and is one of Prince William County's best tax payers, as well as serving its growing population.
Courtesy of the Office of Economic Development

In 1950, a Marine family at Quantico was looking for a house to buy. They found only two houses advertised for sale in the whole of Prince William County, one in Canova and one in Gainesville. In 1960, when suburban building was underway along the interstate corridor, there were 1,113 units available. By 1980, the number had doubled and become 2,598, but the number of occupied units had taken a greater leap from 10,861 to 46,388 in 1980. So much of the growth has taken place in the east of the county that the administrative headquarters has moved again, as so often in the past, to be accessible to the majority. The board of supervisors now meets in the new McCoart Building on Davis Ford Road.[9]
Courtesy of the Office of Economic Development

By the time this photograph of Center Street was taken in 1910, livestock were no longer permitted to roam the unpaved streets. The town had gone into debt to provide the sidewalks and well-graded streets in 1879 and 1885.
Courtesy of the Manassas City Museum

At the same time as they added buildings to meet the needs of a growing population, the citizens of Prince William took steps to see they did not lose the heritage of the past. In 1979 the city of Manassas set apart a historic district. In 1988 the Virginia Division of Historic Landmarks and the National Park Service placed Old Town Manassas on the State and National Registers of Historic Places. In this area are buildings and vistas of the sort familiar to Americans from coast to coast who grew up in small towns begun and augmented from the late nineteenth century to the present.

The county government moved into this Victorian Romanesque building of brick and sandstone in 1894. Since cattle and sheep were still allowed to run at large in town at certain hours at that time, the fence was probably a protective measure.
Courtesy of the Manassas City Museum

Common community entertainments included parades and this crowd of the early auto age appears to be anticipating one in this circa 1910 photograph of Main Street.

The Manassas Town Band provided pleasant memories to those who listened and watched, and to the musicians themselves.
Courtesy of the Manassas City Museum

Along tree-shaded streets like Grant Avenue, life was much more leisurely and placid.
Courtesy of the Manassas City Museum

Manassas had its early movies at the Dixie Theater.
Courtesy of the Manassas City Museum

There were several corner buildings like this in the downtown area. Today this houses restaurants and shops on the first floor, and apartments on the second floor.
Courtesy of the Manassas City Museum

The National Bank at the corner of Center and Main streets was established in 1896.
Courtesy of the Manassas City Museum

Waiting at the depot for the train to Washington, D.C., to shop in town or go to work was done by those willing to make the long ride at the turn of the century.
Courtesy of the Manassas City Museum

The early Orange and Alexandria Railroad had become the Southern Railroad after the Civil War.
Courtesy of the Manassas City Museum

This building alongside the railroad tracks was designed by Albert Speiden for a candy company.
Courtesy of the Manassas City Museum

The cannons near the courthouse were added some years after the Peace Jubilee of 1911. The courts were held in this building until 1984.
Courtesy of the Manassas City Museum

Manassas' town hall and fire station was also designed by Albert Speiden and completed in 1914.
Courtesy of the Manassas City Museum

At about the same time the town acquired public utilities (electricity and water) for which this power plant was constructed. Courtesy of the Manassas City Museum

Cocke's Pharmacy, shown here with its 1940s facade, was the high school congregating spot for the students of Osbourn High in the 1950s. You might not find a seat, one alumna remembered, but the thing to do was to go to visit and be seen. Courtesy of the Manassas City Museum

*This was Manassas' way station for travelers of the motor age.
Courtesy of the Manassas City Museum*

*The Judicial Center remains in Manassas, which is now the site of a division of IBM corporation. IBM ranks as the top employer in the county with a payroll of five thousand people.[10]
Courtesy of the Office of Economic Development*

*The population projection for Prince William County in the year 2000 is between 240,000 and 300,000. Clearly the future is likely to present just as many challenges as the past has done, and the future is moving southward.
Courtesy of Prince William County Historical Commission*

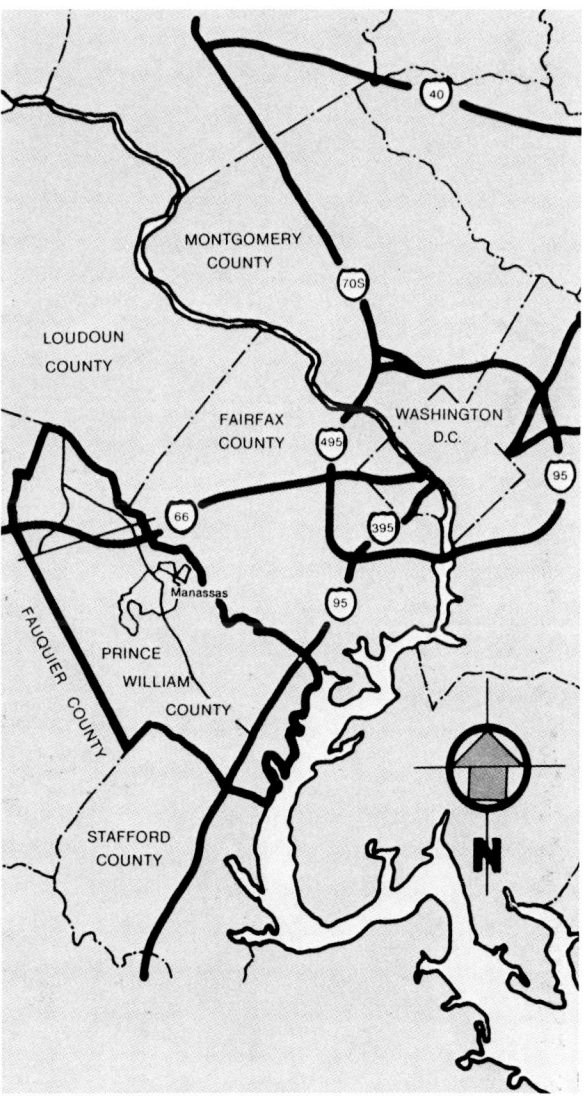

169

Chapter Notes

Chapter 1

1. Michael F. Johnson, "Paleo-Indians: The First Virginians of Fairfax County." *Yearbook: The Historical Society of Fairfax County, Virginia,* Vol. 20, 1984-1985, pp. 5, 6, 12, 13.
2. *Ibid.*, pp. 13-16, and Michael F. Johnson, "The Hunter-Gatherer I Period: Fairfax County 9,000 Years Ago." *The Yearbook: The Historical Society of Fairfax County, Virginia,* Vol. 21, 1986-1988, p. 82; William P. Barse and William M. Gardner, *A Prehistoric Cultural Resources Reconnaissance of Neabsco and Powells Creeks, Prince William County, Virginia,* pp. 12-13; Ronald A. Thomas and James G. Harrison III, *A Phase I Archaeological Survey of Cedar Run, Prince William County, Virginia.*
3. Robert Engelman, "Potowmack Fever." *WETA Magazine,* September, 1988, p. 7; and Robert Engelman, "Washington Before Washington." *Washington Post Sunday Magazine,* July 13, 1986; Stephen Potter, Ph.D., "The Indians of Seventeenth Century Fairfax." *Fairfax Chronicles,* Vol. 7, No. 4, November, 1983.
4. Fairfax Harrison, *Landmarks of Old Prince William: A Study of Origins in Northern Virginia:* Vol. 1 and 2, pp. 21, 24 and 27.
5. *Ibid.*, and p. 59.

Chapter 2

1. Harrison, pp. 46, 54.
2. *Ibid.*, pp. 372-380, and T. H. Breen, *Tobacco Culture: The Mentality of the Great Tidewater Planters on the Eve of the Revolution,* pp. 18-20.
3. *Ibid.*, p. 387.
4. *Ibid.*, p. 142; and Don Curtis, *The Curtis Collection: A Personal View of Prince William County History,* p. 17.
5. William Waller Hening, *The Statutes at Large; Being a collection of all the Laws of Virginia from the First Session of the Legislature in the year 1619,* Vol. 2, pp. 433, 499; Curtis, *ibid.*; interviews with Dr. W. E. S. Flory on May 4, and December 20, 1988, and Bel Air brochure.
6. Harrison, pp. 178-183; Dollye McAlister Elliott, "Nicholas Hayward of London and the Huguenot Emigration to Virginia." *The Colonial Genealogist,* 1976, and George Harrison Sanford King, *The Register of Overwharton Parish, Stafford County, Virginia 1723-1758 and Sundry Historical and Genealogical Notes,* Fredericksburg, Virginia: By the Author, 1961.
7. Interview with Katherine Haynes on April 23, 1988; letters from Mrs. Wigglesworth to James Haynes in possession of Katherine Haynes.
8. Harrison, pp. 239-246.
9. *Ibid.*, 352-364, and Breen, p. 41.
10. Harrison, p. 384, and Breen, p. 62.
11. Lee C. Lansing, Jr., *Historic Dumfries Virginia: Chartered May 11, 1749,* p. 6; and Harrison, pp. 383-385.
12. Typescript of speech to Historic Dumfries association by the Rev. Melvin Lee Steadman, Jr., on June 6, 1974.

Chapter 3

1. Harrison, p. 351; and William J. Serow, *Population of Virginia: Past, Present & Future,* pp. 6-7.
2. Martha Leitch, "Buckland." *Pioneer Papers.*
3. Tommye S. Burton, "Courthouse of Prince William County," *Virginia Cavalcade,* Summer, 1978, pp. 42-44. Early references to Haymarket sometimes use the spelling Haymarket or Hay Market. It is reported there once was a lot of hay sold near the Red House Tavern, nucleus of the town, because of the horse races that were held there in the late eighteenth and early nineteenth century. Robert L. Crewdson, *Crossroads of the Past: A History of Haymarket, Va.* Prince William County Historical Commission, n.d., p. 8.
4. Serow, pp. 5-7.
5. *Ibid.*
6. Writers of the Works Projects Administration in the State of Virginia, *Prince William: The Story of Its People and Its Places,* p. 71. (Hereinafter cited as *WPA Guide*).
7. John Davis, *Travels of Four Years and A Half in the United States of America during 1798, 1799, 1800, 1801 & 1802.* New York: Henry Holt and Company, 1909, pp. 332-336.
8. Interview with Dr. Flory on May 4, 1988.
9. Davis, p. 255
10. Davis, pp. 251-52; Martha Lynn, *A Brief History of Occoquan,* Fredericksburg, Va.: Historic Occoquan, Inc., 1969; and R. Jackson Ratcliffe, *This Was Prince William,* p. 95.
11. Thomas Ellicott, "Description of an improved Mill for grinding corn, as built in Virginia." pp. 319-328, *The Repertory of Arts and Manufactures: consisting of original communications, specification of Patent Inventions, and Selections of Useful Practical Papers from the Transactions of the Philosophical Societies of All Nations, etc., etc.,* Vol. 4, 1796.
12. *Ibid.*, p. 96; and Interview with Hilda Brown Ammerman on November 4, 1988.
13. Tansill family history, typescript.
14. Interview with Virginia Speiden Carper on March 5, 1988.
15. Interview with Wilmer and Mary Porter on October 6, 1988.
16. Interview with Pauline Gossom Padgett on October 21, 1988.
17. *Ibid.*; *WPA Guide,* p. 183, and Madeleine Ginsburg, *An Introduction to Fashion Illustration,* p. 34.
18. Padgett interview; Interview with Hugh Talman, Curator of Black and White Still Photographs, Smithsonian Museum of American History, October 7, 1988; and Nancy Bradfield, *Costume in Detail 1730-1930,* pp. 173, 187.
19. Padgett interview; *WPA Guide,* pp. 46, 187.
20. Interview with Alma Bridge November 6, 1988; *WPA Guide,* p. 172.
21. Dorothy V. Knibb, "Beverly Mills, Broad Road, Virginia: 185-Year-Old Mill Is Still A Going Small Business." *Domestic Commerce,* December 1945, pamphlet reprint.

Chapter 4

1. Robert E. Lee, Jr. Mssl. L51c, folios 852, 853, Virginia Historical Society, Richmond.
2. Knibb, *op. cit.*

Most of the information in this chapter was taken from an overview of the Civil War in Prince William County prepared for the County Planning Office by Historian J. Michael Miller.

Chapter 5

1. George Carr Round, "The Last Signal Message of the War by the One Who Sent It." *Record of the Twenty-Seventh Annual Reunion of the Signal Corps, U.S.A.,* Washington, D.C.: U.S. Veteran Signal Corps Association, 1902.
2. Interview with Virginia Speiden Carper on March 5, 1988; R. Jackson Ratcliff, *This Was Manassas,* p. 53; and Lynn, pp. 8-9.
3. Elizabeth Harrover Johnson, E. R. Conner III, and Mary Harrover Ferguson, *History in a Horseshoe Curve: The Story of Sudley Methodist Church and Its Community,* p. 180.
4. Ratcliffe, *This Was Manassas,* p. 49.
5. Interview with Annie Bailey Rose on October 25, 1988; *WPA Guide,* pp. 146-47.
6. Sister M. Helen Johnston, *The Fruit of His Works: A History of the Benedictine Sisters of St. Benedict's Convent, Bristow, Prince William County, Virginia,* pp. 37-38, 48, 55, 61-62, 78, 87-88, 96 and 101; Interview with Sister Anita Sherwood, OSB, on December 19, 1988.

7. Bergen and Cornelia Evans, *Dictionary of Contemporary American Usage,* p. 322.
8. Anne P. Flory, "Richard Stoddert Ewell." Typescript of a speech given to Historic Dumfries on June 2, 1977. Mrs. Flory reported that, in correspondence among the Ewells before the Civil War, family members referred to the farm near Nokesville where General Ewell spent his boyhood as "Stony Lonesome."
9. Ratcliffe, *This Was Prince William,* p. 102.

Chapter 6, Part 1

Material in this section is based on Lt. Col. Charles A. Fleming, *et al, Quantico: Crossroads of the Marine Corps;* an interview with retired Marine officer Edward Stallknecht on June 29, 1988, and an article in the *Washington Star,* May 14, 1967.

Chapter 6, Part 2

1. Manassas *Journal Messenger Centennial Edition 1869-1969,* p. 7.
2. Interview with Hattie Mae Partlow on September 6, 1988.
3. Interviews with Pauline Padgett and Margaret Callander on October 21, 1988; *WPA Guide,* p. 183.
4. *Washington Post,* Thursday, November 3, 1977, p. VA 3 "Church Rescued from Demolition," and Janna Lee Murphy Leepson, "Bethel Church." An address presented at a meeting of Historic Dumfries, Virginia, Inc. at the Dumfries Town Hall, January 8, 1981.
5. Leepson, *Ibid.,* Interviews with Janna Lee Murphy Leepson on September 24, 1988, and with Galen Garber on October 6, 1988; and Virginia Historic Landmarks Commission Survey Form, File 76, Russell House and Store, by Frances Johnson, September 1, 1982.

Chapter 6, Part 3

1. Harrison, p. 486.
2. *Ibid.,* pp. 455, 463.
3. Charles Gilles, *A History of the Greenwich Presbyterian Church.* The crack in the glass at lower left of the picture indicates this is an early form of photography called Ambrotype in which the glass negative became the print by painting or pasting dark color on the back. The process was popular in the 1850s, so this could be the first picture taken of the church immediately after it was built in 1858. All subsequent pictures show the church as red brick.
4. Anne Green, *With Much Love,* pp. 57-58.
5. Julian Green, *Memories of Happy Days,* p. 1.
6. Personal communication Grace Dulin, granddaughter of the Rev. B. P. Dulin, to James Cooke, quoted in a letter to the author dated August 24, 1988.

Chapter 6, Part 4

1. Edith Moore Sprouse, *Colchester: Colonial Port on the Potomac,* Fairfax, Virginia: Fairfax County Office of Comprehensive Planning, 1975, pp. 85, 88; and Charles Lee Lewis, *Famous American Marines,* Boston: L. C. Page & Company, 1950, p. 75, quoted in Sprouse.
2. Manassas *Journal,* September 24, 1931.
3. Eileen Mead, "The restoration of Rippon Lodge." *Potomac News,* October 8, 1971.
4. The Society of the Cincinnati was formed by the officers who served with General Washington in the Continental Line during the Revolution. Only one descendent of each of the original members may belong at any one time. The headquarters of the Cincinnati, Anderson House in Washington, D.C., is also a museum. The flag Admiral Black held in the picture is displayed there.
Information in this section was based on interviews with Christopher Brown on July 29, 1988, Hilda Cline Brown Ammerman on November 4, 1988, Hilary "Pete" Costello, on June 29, 1988, Agnes Webster on April 24, 1988, Ellis Hawkins on June 29, 1988, and Rear Adm. and Mrs. R. B. Black on July 29, 1988 and September 24, 1988.

Chapter 7, part 1

1. Susan Cary Strickland, *Prince William Forest Park: An Administrative History,* p. 7.
2. Washington *Star,* March 6, 1935; Dr. Charles W. Porter, "Preliminary Historical Report on Chopawamsic, SP-22, Virginia." Harrison, p. 52.
3. U.S. Department of the Interior, *Recreational Demonstration Projects,* n.d.
4. Porter, *Ibid.,* pp. 8 and 16.
5. *Ibid.*
6. Interview with Annie Williams on July 18, 1988; Strickland, pp. 12-13, and Ronald L. Heinemann, *Depression and New Deal in Virginia: The Enduring Dominion,* pp. 121-122.
7. Parker, p. 128; Strickland, p. 8; Interview with Barbara Kirby March 2, 1988.

Chapter 7, Part 3

1. Kermit Roosevelt, *War Report of the OSS (Office of Strategic Services),* p. 211.
2. *Ibid.,* p. 241.
3. National Archives, Record Group 226, Box 538.
4. *Ibid.,* Box 158.
5. Strickland, p. 28.

Chapter 7, Part 4

1. *Ibid.,* pp. 32-34.
1. Ira B. Lykes, "Report of Seasonal Camp Operations 1950." Prince William Forest Park, Triangle, Virginia, unpublished manuscript.
3. Parker, *Ibid.,* p. 151.

Chapter 8, Part 1

1. Larry Van Dyne, "The Making of Washington." *Washingtonian,* pp 204-208.
2. Donald E. Curtis, *The Curtis Collection: A Personal View of Prince William County History,* pp. 20-21; Goldie Keys Brawner and Ann Hoagland, personal communication, December 30, 1988.
3. Katherine Cole Stevenson and H. Ward Jandl, *Houses by Mail: A Guide to Houses from Sears, Roebuck & Company,* Washington, D.C.: p. 64.
4. Interview with Ruth Round Hooff and Althea Hooff Cooksey on April 28, 1988, and George C. Round, "Miramne of Belle Aire," typescript.
5. Washington *Star,* June 16, 1961, and Interview with Wilmer and Mary Porter on October 6, 1988.

Chapter 8, Part 2

1. J. Birchfield "Haymarket Homesites: Estate to Become Country Club," *Evening Star,* December 6, 1968; Dick Slay, "Tradition Lives at Evergreen." *Evening Star,* September 29, 1974; *Evening Star* ad February 11, 1967.
2. Prince William County Historical Commission, *Prince William: A Past to Preserve,* p. 22.
3. Manassas *Journal Messenger: Centennial Edition 1869-1969,* May 1969, "County Was Once A Major Milk Producer," History and Farming Section, p. 7.
4. Interview with Ellis Hawkins on June 29, 1988.
5. Interviews with J. Howard Joynt on December 12, 1988 and Martha Joynt Kumar on December 11, 1988.
6. Interviews with W. A. Hampton, Jr., on July 11, 1988 and Allen Dent, Jr., on July 19, 1988.
7. Interview with Karen White on July 19, 1988.
8. Paul Hodge, "1984 Start Urged for Park on Potomac." Washington *Post.*
9. "Prince William County Data" (pamphlet).
10. *Ibid.*

Bibliography

Books

Barse, William P. and William M. Gardner. *A Prehistoric Cultural Resources Reconnaissance of Neabsco and Powells Creeks, Prince William County, Virginia.* Prince William, Virginia: Prepared by Thunderbird Research Corporation, Front Royal, Virginia.

Bradfield, Nancy. *Costume in Detail 1730-1930.* New Edition. Boston: Plays, Inc., 1968, 1981.

Breen, T. H. *Tobacco Culture: The Mentality of the Great Tidewater Planters on the Eve of Revolution.* Princeton, New Jersey: Princeton University Press, 1985.

Civilian Conservation Corps. *Official Annual 1937 District 3: Third Corps Area.*

Clark, Annye Beatrix and Catherine Smith Arrington. *History of Prince William County.* Second Edition. Prince William County, Virginia: County School Board, 1933.

Conner, Edgar Ren III. *On Time to Monroe: Legend and Lore of the Southern Railway, Washington Division.* Revised second edition. Manassas, Virginia: By the author, 1980.

Curtis, Donald E. *The Curtis Collection: A Personal View of Prince William County History.* Prince William, Virginia: Prince William County Historical Commission, 1988.

Evans, Bergen and Cornelia Evans. *A Dictionary of Contemporary American Usage.* New York: Random House, 1957.

Ewell, Alice Maude. *A Virginia Scene or Life in Old Prince William.* Lynchburg, Virginia: J. P. Bell Co., Inc., Publishers, 1931.

Fleming, Lt. Col. Charles A., Capt. Robin L. Austin, and Capt. Charles A. Braley III. *Quantico: Crossroads of the Marine Corps.* Washington, D.C.: History and Museums Divisions, USMC, 1978.

Gewehr, Wesley M. *The Great Awakening in Virginia 1740-1790.* Gloucester, Massachusetts: Peter Smith, 1965. (Reprint of Duke University Press publication, 1930).

Ginsburg, Madeleine. *An Introduction to Fashion Illustration.* London: Pitman Publishing Ltd., 1980.

Green, Anne. *With Much Love.* New York: Harper & Brothers Publishers, 1948.

Green, Julian. *Memories of Happy Days.* New York & London: Harper & Brothers, Publishers, 1942.

Griffin, William E., Jr. *One Hundred Fifty Years of History Along the Richmond, Fredericksburg and Potomac Railroad.* Richmond, Virginia: RF&P RR, 1984. (Compiled from a series in the RF&P "Rail-O-Gram")

Harrison, Fairfax. *Landmarks of Old Prince William: A Study of Origins in Northern Virginia.* Vols. 1-2. Baltimore: Prince William County Historical Commission, 1987.

Heinemann, Ronald L. *Depression and New Deal in Virginia, The Enduring Dominion.* Charlottesville, Virginia: The University Press of Virginia, 1983.

Henderson, William D. *The Road to Bristoe Station: Campaigning with Lee and Meade, August 1—October 20, 1863.* Lynchburg, Virginia: By the author, 1987.

Hening, William Waller, ed. *The Statutes at Large: Being a Collection of all the Laws of Virginia from the First Session of the Legislature in the Year 1619.* Vols. 1-3. New York: By the editor, 1823.

Johnson, Elizabeth Harrover, E. R. Conner III, and Mary Harrover Ferguson. *History in a Horseshoe Curve: The Story of Sudley Methodist Church and Its Community.* Princeton, New Jersey: By the authors, 1982.

Johnson, Elizabeth Harrover. *Sea Change: A Biography.* Princeton, New Jersey: By the author, 1977.

Johnston, Sister M. Helen, OSB, BS. *The Fruit of His Works: A History of the Benedictine Sisters of St. Benedict's Convent, Bristow, Prince William County, Virginia.* Bristow, Virginia: Linton Hall Press, 1953.

Mackall, William W. *A Son's Recollection of His Father.* New York: E. P. Dutton, Inc., 1930.

Naisawald, VanLoan. *Manassas Junction & The Doctor.* Manassas, Virginia: By the author, 1981.

Nelson, Tom. *An Oral History: an interview with Rosemary Selecman "Occoquan's Friend."* Prince William, Virginia: Prince William County Historical Commission Oral History Project, 1980.

Parker, Patricia. *The Hinterland: An Overview of the Prehistory and History of Prince William Forest Park, Virginia.* Washington, D.C.: U.S. Department of the Interior, National Park Service, 1986.

Prince William County Historical Commission. *Prince William: A Past to Preserve.* Prince William, Virginia: Prince William County Historical Commission, 1982.

Ratcliffe, R. Jackson. *This Was Manassas.* Manassas, Virginia: By the author, 1973.

Ratcliffe, R. Jackson. *This Was Prince William.* Leesburg, Virginia: Potomac Press, 1978.

Roosevelt, Kermit. *War Report of the OSS (Office of Strategic Services)* Prepared by History Projects Strategic Services Unit Office of the Assistant Secretary of War, War Department, Washington, D.C. Declassified portion published by authority July 17, 1975. New York: Walker & Co., 1976.

Serow, William J. *Population of Virginia: Past, Present & Future.* Charlottesville, Virginia: University of Virginia Press, 1978.

Simmons, Catherine T. *Manassas, Virginia 1873-1973: One Hundred Years of a Virginia Town.* Manassas, Virginia: Manassas City Museum, 1986.

Stevenson, Katherine Cole and H. Ward Jandl. *Houses by Mail: A Guide to Houses from Sears, Roebuck & Company.* Washington, D.C.: National Trust For Historic Preservation, 1986.

Strickland, Susan Cary. *Prince William Forest Park: An Administrative History.* Washington, D.C.: History Division, National Park Service, 1986.

Templeman, Eleanor and Nan Netherton. *Northern Virginia Heritage.* New York: Avenel Books, 1966.

Rabatin, June, ed. *Count the Ties to Manassas.* Manassas, Virginia: The Manassas Museum, 1984.

Thomas, Ronald A. and James G. Harrison III. *A Phase I Archaeological Survey of Cedar Run, Prince William County, Virginia.* Prince William County Government.

U.S. Department of Commerce. Bureau of the Census. Norman Cousins, Honorary Editor. *Reflections of America: Commemorating the Statistical Abstract Centennial.* Washington, D.C.: 1980.

Writers Program, Works Project Administration in Virginia. *Prince William: The Story of Its People and Its Places.* Bicentennial Edition. Manassas, Virginia. The Bethlehem Good Housekeeping Club, 1976. (Originally compiled 1941.)

Newspapers and Periodicals

Arnold, James R. "Leesylvania State Park." *Northern Virginia Heritage*. Vol. 7, No. 3. October 1985. pp. 11-15.

Barlow, M. R. "History of the Prince William Cavalry." *Confederate Veteran*. Vol. 15, August 1907. pp. 353-355.

Beahm, Early, Ralph, Charles and Robert. *Looking Back: Some Accounts of Bygone Years*. (Pamphlet) Nokesville, Virginia: By the authors, 1988.

Burton, Tommye S. "Courthouses of Prince William County, Virginia." *Cavalcade*. Summer 1978. pp. 34-47.

Ellicott, Thomas. Description of an improved Mill for grinding corn, as built in Virginia." *The Repertory of Arts and Manufactures: consisting of original communications, specifications of Patent Inventions, and Selections of Useful Practical Papers from the Transactions of the Philosphical Societies of all Nations, etc. etc.* Vol. 4. London: 1796.

Elliott, Dollye McAlister. "Nicholas Hayward of London and the Huguenot Emigration to Virginia." *The Colonial Genealogist*. 1976.

Engelman, Robert. "Potowmack Fever." *WETA Magazine*. September 1988.

___. "Washington Before Washington." *Washington Post Sunday Magazine*. July 13, 1986.

Hodge, Paul. "1984 Start Urged for Park on Potomac." *Washington Post*. July 13, 1983.

Hotz, Robert B. "Amelia Earhart (1897-1937)." *World Book Encyclopedia*. Vol. 6. Chicago: Field Enterprises Educational Corporation, 1965.

Johnson, Michael F. "Paleo-Indians: The First Virginians of Fairfax County." *Historical Society of Fairfax County Yearbook*. Vol. 20, 1984-85. pp. 5-18.

"The Hunter-Gatherer I Period: Fairfax County 9,000 Years Ago." *Historical Society of Fairfax County Yearbook*. Vol. 21, 1986-88. pp. 74-84.

Knibb, Dorothy V. "Beverly Mills, Broad Road, Virginia: 185-Year-Old Mill Is Still a Going Small Business." *Domestic Commerce*. December 1945. (Pamphlet reprint).

Lackey, Patrick K. "Man of Unity: Dumfries in Vanguard on Racial Harmony." *The Virginian-Pilot*. June 7, 1988, p. 1

Lansing, Lee C., Jr. *Historic Dumfries, Virginia. Chartered 11 May 1749*. Dumfries, Virginia: Historic Dumfries, Virginia, Inc., 1974.

Leitch, Martha. "Buckland." *Echoes of History*. Vol. 3, No. 6. Publication of the Pioneer America Society. November 1973.

Lynn, Martha R. *A Brief History of Occoquan: Established 1804*. (pamphlet c. 1975.)

Mead, Eileen. "No time to die: Annie Shumate, 89, loves what she's lived." *Potomac News*, May 23, 1978.

"Old Days on the farm recreated in model." *Potomac News*. November 29, 1972.

"Over 50 years of 'Friendship, love and truth.'" *Potomac News*. September 1, 1971.

"The Restoration of Rippon Lodge." *Potomac News*. October 8, 1971.

Potter, Stephen R., Ph.D. "The Indians of Seventeenth Century Fairfax." *Fairfax Chronicles*. Vol. 7, No. 4. November 1983-January 1984.

Prince William County. "Prince William County Data." (Pamphlet) July 1987.

Round, George C. "History of Manassas." *Manassas Journal*. May 21, 1897.

Shepherd, Hazel Bowman. "Nokesville—Our Town—A Pictorial History." Pamphlet published for Nokesville Day, June 4, 1977 by the Nokesville, Virginia Ruritan Club.

Templeman, Eleanor Lee. "The Lees of Leesylvania." *Northern Virginia Heritage*. Vol. 7, No. 3. October 1985. pp. 17-19.

Van Dyne, Larry. "The Making of Washington." *Washingtonian*. November 1987.

Wallace, Jerry, The Rev. "A Parson At Large: Being an Account of Mason Locke Weems, George Washington's Quaint Biographer, and his Relation to the American Episcopate." (Pamphlet) Springfield, Illinois: By the author, 1927, 1934.

Washington *Evening Star*. "Recreation Park Planned in Nearby Virginia." March 6, 1935.

Washington Post. "Restoration." (of Rockledge, Occoquan). April 6, 1974.

Watson, Douglas. "Adventure Is His Daily Diet." *Washington Post*. July 4, 1968.

Willman, John B. "Five Builders Committed: Community Linked to Lake." *Washington Post* Real Estate, D1. November 8, 1969.

Wills, Mary Alice. *"Confederate Batteries Along the Potomac."* Prince William, Virginia. Prince William County Historical Commission, June 1967. (Pamphlet Reprint.)

Addresses, Manuscripts and Unpublished Reports

Black, Richard Blackburn. "Rippon Lodge and the Blackburns." An address presented at a meeting of Historic Dumfries, Virginia, Inc. at the Dumfries Town Hall, October 3, 1974.

Flory, William E. S., Ph.D. "Parson Weems—First Biographer of Washington." An address presented at a meeting of Historic Dumfries February 6, 1975.

"Parson Weems—Marketer." Address to Historic Dumfries February 3, 1977.

"Mason Locke Weems—Cleric." An address to Historic Dumfries April 8, 1974.

Gerner, Charles H., Project Manager. "Chopawamsic VA Project Report—Preliminary Proposal." unpublished manuscript c. 1932-33.

Gossom, Elizabeth Owens Smith. "A History of the Family and Ancestors of Mrs. Richard Benoni Gossom as recorded by her about 1939." (typescript).

Leepson, Janna Lee Murphy. "Bethel Church." Address prsented to Historic Dumfries January 8, 1981.

Lykes, Ira, Manager. *Prince William Forest Park*. Washington, D.C.: National Capitol Parks, U.S. National Park Service, U.S. Department of Interior, c. 1946.

Miller, J. Michael. "National Register of Historic Places Multiple Property Documentation Form." Prepared for Prince William County, Virginia for submission to the State Registrar of Historic Landmarks, 1988.

Porter, Dr. Charles W. "Preliminary Historical Report on Chopawamsic, SP-22, Virginia." unpublished manuscript dated December 28, 1935.

Russell House and Store, Minnieville Road, Occoquan. Virginia Historic Landmarks Survey File #76 dated September 1, 1982.

Round, George Carr. *Glimpses of George Carr Round*. Manassas, Virginia: Published by his daughter Ruth Round Hoff on the occasion of the dedication of the George C. Round Elementary School, 1986.

Tansill Family History. Unpublished typescript.

Oral History

(All interviews were done in 1988 unless otherwise noted.)
Ammerman, Hilda Cline Brown on November 4.
Beahm, Robert and Aileen on September 12.
Black, RADM and Mrs. R. B. on July 22 and September 24.
Brown, Christopher on July 29.
Carper, Virginia Speiden on March 5.
Cooke, James L. on March 6 and June 26.
Cooksey, Althea Hooff on April 28.
Costello, Hilary on June 29.
Davis, Frances Hinson on July 29.
Dent, Allen, Jr. on July 19.
Ferguson, Mary Harrover on October 21.
Flory, Dr. W. E. S. on May 4 and September 24.
Garber, Galen on October 6.
Gnadt, C. E., Clerk of the County Court, on August 8.
Hampton, William A., Jr., on July 11.
Hawkins, Ellis on June 29.
Haynes, Katherine on April 23.
Hooff, Ruth Round on April 28.
Joynt, J. Howard on December 12.
King, Supervisor Ed on November 4.
Kirby, Barbara on March 2.
Klakowitz, James on March 30.
Leepson, Janna Lee Murphy on September 24.
MacDonald, G. E. and Jane on April 30.
Padgett, Barton and Pauline on October 21.
Partlow, Hattie Mae on August 8 and September 6.
Porter, Wilmer and Mary on October 6.
Rose, Annie Bailey on October 25.
Stallknecht, Edward on June 29.
Townsend, Jan on July 18.
Webster, Agnes on April 24.
White, Karen on July 19.
Williams, Annie Thomas on July 18.

INDEX

A
Albany, Treaty of, 14, 17
Alexandria, 25
Algonquins, 10
Allen, Epp, 88
Ambrotype, 30
Annaburg Manor, 52, 76
Antioch Baptist Church, 31
Army of the Potomac, 43
Avon Farm, 44

B
Bacon Race Church, 81
Baldwin House, later Baldwin Hall, 55
Ball, Alfred, 39, 40
Baptist Church, Manassas, 51
Baptists, "Hard Shelled," 81
Bates, Betsy, 29
Batestown, 29
Bauckman, Sam, 134
Beahm, Alverta Early, 63
Beahm, Charles, 63
Beahm, Cora, 63
Beahm, Early, 63
Beahm, Ella, 63
Beahm, George W., 60, 63
Beahm, Hazel. *See* Bucher
Beahm, Isaac Newton Harvey, Professor, 63
Beahm, Ralph, 63
Beahm, Robert, 63
Beahm, Rosa Lee. *See* Rankin
Beale, Fanny, 33
Bel Air, 12, 136-37
Belle of Leesylvania, 19
Berkeley, Ed, Col., 142
Berkeley, Lewis, 143
Bethel Methodist Church, 82-83
Bittle, C. O., 80
Black, Avisa, 100
Black, Douglas, 100
Black, Martha, 139
Black, Richard Blackburn, Rear Adm., 100
Black population, 24-25
Blackburn, Richard, 14, 97, 100

Boone, Daniel, 100
Brawner, Charles, 131
Brawner, Goldie Keys, 134
Brawner, Johnnie, 131
Brawner, Randolph, 136, 138
Brent Town Tract, 16
Brentsville (town), 22, 29, 34, 48
Brentsville Academy, 57
Brentsville Court House, 94
Brentsville District High (Nokesville), 78-79
Brethren (German Baptists, sometimes called Dunkards), 58-61
Broad Run, 29, 33
Brooks, Elias, 88
Brown Field, Quantico, 70
Brown, Lt. Walter, 70
Brown, William, 142
Brown, William F., Gen., 68
Bucher, Hazel Beahm, 63
Buckland, 22, 31
Buckland Tavern, 31
Buckland, William, 22
Bull Run tract, 24
Butler, Smedley, Maj. Gen., 72, 109

C
Cabin Branch Mine, 106
Cabin camps, 114, 116
Carolina Road, 16, 22, 32, 87
Carper, Virginia Speiden, 28
Catawbas, 10
Catharpin, 55
Catharpin School, 77
Cedar Hill farm, 25, 27, 105
Chapman, Jonathan, 33
Cherokees, 10
Cherry Hill peninsula, 17
Chinn House, 37
Chopawamsic Recreation Demonstration Area, 104, 112, 118, 122
Chubb, Percy, 149
Cincinnati, Society of, 100
Civil War, 34-46
Civilian Conservation Corps, 110, 112, 114, 116

Clarke, John W., 135
Clarke, Mamie V., 135
Clarkson, Dr., 142
Cleary, Paul, 139
Cline, Annie. *See* Annie Keys Shumate
Cline, David, Dr., 92
Clover Hill Farm, 74
Commercial fishing, 154
Costello, Brad, 93
Costello, Hilary "Pete," 93
Costello, Steve, 94
Court houses (district and county), 22
Crawford, Dellie, 131
Crumpacker, Daisy Early, 58
Curtis, Don, 157

D
Dairy Festival. *See* Piedmont Dairy Festival
Davis, John, 23, 24
Davis, Mary Early, 58
Dean, Jennie, 48, 55, 56
Deep Hole Plantation, 15
DePauw, Newland, Col., 142
"Dinky" railroad, 108
Dodd, Will, 88
Dodge, William, 142
Donovan, William J., Gen., 118
Duck hunting at Leesylvania, 148-155
Dulin, B. P., Rev., 88
Dumfries, 14, 17, 19, 22, 25, 90, 128, 130-139
Dunkards. *See* Brethren
Dunlop, William, 19

E
Early, Alverta. *See* Beahm
Early, Daisy. *See* Crumpacker
Early, Ella. *See* Flory
Early, Martha Miller "Mattie," 58
Early, Mary. *See* Davis
Early, Michael G., 58-59
Early, Ola. *See* Herring
East View Farm, 59
Eastern College, 55
Education. *See* Brentsville Academy,

Brentsville District High School, Catharpin School, Eastern College, Hebron Seminary, Linton Hall School, Manassas Academy, Manassas (Osbourn) High, Manassas Vocational Industrial School for Colored Youth, St. Edith's, St. Anne's, Swavely School
Effingham, 144
Ellicott, Thomas, 25-26
Ellicott's Mill, 25-26, 92
Ellis, W. H., Mrs., 97, 101
Ellis, Wade Hampton, Judge, 97
Emory Farm, 147
English colonial trade policy, 14
Episcopal Church, Dumfries, 134
Evergreen, 143
Ewell, Fannie, 28
Ewell, Frances, 23
Ewell, Jesse, Col., 23
Ewell, Richard S., 28. *See also* Stony Lonesome

F
Fairfax House, Leesylvania, 18
Flory, Anne, 137
Flory, Ella Early, 58
Flory, William E. S., Professor, 136-37
Foley, Annie. *See* Smith
Foley, Nancy Randolph Mallory, 30
Foley, William, 31
Foley, Willis, 30
Fort, colonial on Neabsco Creek, 12
Four-H Club class, 83
Fraley, Ed, 138-39
Freestone Point Hunt Club, 150-51
Freestone Point Recreation Center, 155
Freestone, S.S., 155-56
Fun Farm, Manassas, 145

G
Gallahand, Cosmo, 131
Garber, Galen, 83
Garrison, Cecil, 136, 138
Garrison, J. K., 139
Garrison's Store, 131-32
Gay, Leighanna, 154
Girl Scout campers at Mawavi, 124
Glasgow trading firms, 19. *See also* Scottish merchants
Grayson, William, 22
Great Warriors Path, 10
Green, Anne, 84
Green, Charles, 84
Green, Julian, 84
Greenwich, 86-89
Greenwich Presbyterian Church, 87
Grinstead, 28

H
Hagley, 33
Hampton, Barbara, 154
Hampton, Delores, 154
Hampton, William A. "Butch," Jr., 148-49
Hampton, William A. "Doc," 148, 153-54
Hawkins, Alice, 99
Hawkins, Clegget, 99
Hawkins, Edward, 99
Hawkins, Ellis, 99
Haymarket, 22, 32
Haymarket Agricultural Club, 142
Haynes, James, 15, 17-19
Hayward, Nicholas, 16
Hebron Seminary, 58-61
Heineken, Christian, 142

Henderson, Alexander, 92
Henderson, Archibald, 22, 92
Henderson, Bertie. *See* Kyer
Henderson, Cleve, 106
Henderson House, 92
Henderson, Norman, 106
Henderson, Provie, 106
Henderson, Robert, 106
Henderson Village, 135
Henson, Louis, 142
Herring, Ola Early, 58
Herris, William, 15
Hersch, Mabel Harley "Grannie," 145
Hersch, Orville, 145
Hickory Ridge, 107
Hill, J. Carl, 155
Hoadley, 81
Hodge, B. Templeton, Professor, 55
Hooker, J. A., 60
Hotels. *See* Buckland Tavern, Prince William Hotel, Stonewall Jackson Hotel, Summit House, and Williams Ordinary
Huguenots, 16
Hulfish, Thomas, 152-53

I
Indians, 10, 11, 14, 15, 16, 17
Inspection of tobacco, 14, 19
Interstate 95, 15
Iroquois, 10, 17

J
Janney, Eli, H., 142
Janney brothers' mill in Occoquan, 25
Jefferson, Thomas, 22
Jewish Community Center campers, 124
Johnson, Louise, 83
Johnson, Rutland, 74
Joynt, J. Howard, 151, 153, 155
Joynt, Martha. *See* Kumar

K
Katsarelis, Nick, 138
Kendall, Charles Frank, 106
Kendall, John, 108
Kendall, Warfield, 106
Kettle Run, 43
Keys, Annie McCracken, 25, 27, 92, 105
Keys, Annie G. *See* Shumate
Keys, B., farm outside Dumfries, 130
Keys, Elmirah Liming, 105
Keys, Elvan F., 98, 105
Keys, Eunice, 105
Keys, Evandon George Washington, 105
Keys, Goldie. *See* Brawner
Keys, Hannah, 105
Keys, James Isaac, 105
Keys, Katie, 105
Keys, Magruder, 25, 92, 105
Keys, Owen, 105
Keys, Paul Reid, 105
Keys, Ruth L., 105
Keys, Vanetta Mary, 105
Keys, William Francis, 105
King, Robert, 131
Kinnard, Frank, 152-53
Kumar, Martha Joynt, 151
Kyer, Bertie Henderson, 106

L
La Chapelle Restaurant, Manassas, 54
La Grange, 31
Lawn, The, 84, 86
Leach, Beverly, 88

Leach, Murray, 88
Lee, Henry II, 18
Lee, Henry "Light Horse Harry," 22
Lee, Lucy Grymes, 18
Leesylvania, 18, 92, 148, 157, 161
Lejeune, John, Maj. Gen., 70
Leppert, Fred, 81
Liberia (home), 48-49
Linton, Sarah, 56
Linton Hall School, 56
Lintonsford, 56
Lowe, Andrew, 142
Ludwig, Daniel K., 157
Lykes, Ira B., 119

M
McCracken, Annie. *See* Keys
McInter, Charles, 131
Manahoac, 10
Manassas, 27, 48, 51, 76, 163-69
Manassas Academy, 48
Manassas Gap Railroad, 33, 54
Manassas High School, 80
Manassas Junction, 34, 41-42, 48
Manassas National Battlefield Park, 145
Manassas Vocational Industrial School for Colored Youth, 48, 56
Manasseh's Gap, 25
Mann, William Hodges, Gov., 53
Marine Corps Schools, 70-71
Marion, Gus, 97
Marion, Tom, 97
Marumsco Village, 157
Mason, George, Col., 14-15
Mason, George (of Gunston Hall), 19, 22
Merchant, Annie, 138
Merchant, Violet, 138
Mills. *See* Chapman's, Ellicott's, and Nelson's
Mine Road, 108
Moonshine, 109
Mosby's Rangers, 36, 44-45
Mount Atlas (home), 30
Mount Atlas Lane, 33
Mountain View Farm, 78
Mountjoy, Alton, 139
Mountjoy, Willard, 139
Moxley, Aminta Douglass, 87
Moxley, Gilbert Ireland, 87
Murphy, Janna Lee, 83
"My Son John," 54

N
Neabsco Creek, 12, 15, 155
Nelson, Bettie Weedon, 29, 50
Nelson, Edwin, 29, 50
Nelson, Effie. *See* Speiden
Nelson, Elizabeth. *See* Weedon
Nelson, James Edwin, 50
Nelson, John Horatio, 50
Nelson, Paul, 50
Nelson, Thomas, 28
New Deal economic measures, 104
Nokesville, 58-61

O
Occoquan (river ferry), 15
Occoquan (town), 20, 22, 25, 44
Occoquan District High School, 92
Odd Fellow Hall, Dumfries, 131
Office of Special Services, 116, 118, 119
Oil derrick, Nokesville, 60
Old Red School, Greenwich, 89

Orange and Alexandria Railroad (map), 25, 34, 48
Osbourn High School, Manassas, 80

P
Paleo Indians, 10
Palmer, Brenda, 83
Peters, Franz, 142
Peters, Rose, 14
Pickett, Ann Matilda Smith, 33
Pickett, Katherine Ann, 33
Piedmont Dairy Festival, 76
Pohick Church (Powheek), 23
Pohle, Julius, Father, 56
Points, Indian artifacts, 11
Porter, Gwendolyn. *See* Washington
Porter, Hazel. *See* Scites
Porter, Mary, 139
Porter, Wilmer, 129, 138-39
Portici, 39
Portner, Robert and Anna, 52
Possum Point, 146
Possum Point Hunt Club, 147
Possum Point Power Station, 148, 162
Potomac Company, 68
Potomac Path, 12, 19, 130, 134
Potomac River Blockade, 36
Potter, Stephen, 10
Powell's Creek, 155
Presbyterian Church, Manassas, 54
Price, Bowman, 142
Prince William Court House, Manassas, 162
Prince William Forest Park, 25, 28-29, 104-119
Prince William Hotel, 54
Prince William Normal School, 57
Prince William Resolves, 19
Puffenbarger, Shirley, 83
Pyrite mine, 29, 106, 108

Q
Quakers (Society of Friends), 24-25
Quantico (town), 72
Quantico Company, 68
Quantico Creek, 19, 22
Quantico Creek Garage, 135
Quantico Marine Base, 68-73

R
Railroad Post Office, 54
Ratcliffe, George, 131
Richmond, Fredericksburg and Potomac Railroad, 146, 148
Rippon Lodge, 18, 97-98, 101
Roadbuilding equipment (CCC), 112

Robinson, James, 40
Robnel, 50
Rockledge, 24
Rose, Annie Bailey, 56
Round, George Carr, 36, 46, 48, 53
Russell, G. C., 83

S
St. Anne's, 55-56
St. Benedict, Sister of the Order of, 56
St. Edith's, 55-56
St. Paul's Episcopal Church, Haymarket, 33
Scarlett, Martin, 15
Scites, Hazel Porter, 139
Scites, Ronald, 139
Scottish merchants, 14
Sears-Roebuck house, Dumfries, 134
Shumate, Albert, Rev., 27, 92
Shumate, Annie Keys Cline, 92
Slavery, 24-25, 30, 55
Smith, Annie Foley, 33
Smith, Florence Burroughs, 33
Southern Railroad, 166
Speakes, Clay, 131
Speiden, Albert, 50-51, 167
Speiden, Effie Nelson, 50
Speiden, Virginia. *See* Carper
Spotswood, Alexander, Gov., 14, 17
Stagecoach Inn. *See* Williams Ordinary
Stonewall Jackson Hotel, Manassas, 54
Stoney Lonesome, 59
Sudley Ford, 38
Sudley Methodist Church, 38
Summit House, 57
Sunnyside Episcopal Mission, 89
Surveyor's House, Leesylvania, 18
Swaveley School, 55

T
Taft, William Howard, Pres., 53
Tansill, Fannie Weems, 28
Tansill, Robert, 27-28, 50
Tayloe, John, Col., 15
Taylor, Estelle, 106
Taylor, Jennie, 106
Taylor, John Woodward, 106
Taylor, L. Paul, 68
Taylor, Robert, 106
Tebbs, Willoughby house, 90, 133
Templeman, Eleanor Lee, 157
Thomas, Anita. *See* Triplett
Thomas, Annie. *See* Williams
Thomas, George W., 107
Thomas, Nancy Sims, 107
Thornton's Tavern, Greenwich, 86

Tobacco trade, regulation, 14, 19
Topography of northern Virginia, changing, 8-11
Towns, colonial beginning, 14
Triangle, 113
Triplett, Anita Thomas, 106
Turner, Thomas C., Col., 70

U
U.S. Marine Corps, 66-73. *See also* Archibald Henderson and Robert Tansill

V
Van Pelt, Abraham, 41
Virginia Power, 146

W
Washington, Clyde, 139
Washington, Gwendolyn Porter, 139
Washington, Malcolm, 88
Washington City, 34
Waterfall Post Office, 81
Waterfall Road, 33
Warrenton Turnpike Road, 25, 31
Waters, Ed, 138
Waters, Ella, 131
Waters, Reuel, 138
Waverly, 142
Webster, Agnes, 95-96
Weedon, Austin, 50
Weedon, Austin (the younger), 50
Weedon, Bettie. *See* Nelson
Weedon, Elizabeth, 50
Weedon, Elizabeth Nelson, 50
Weems, Fannie. *See* Tansill
Weems, Mason Locke, Rev., 23-24
Weems-Botts House Museum, 17, 23, 137
Weir family, 48
Wheat, Kloman, 136
Wheelock, William H., 148-49
White, William "Billy" Wesley, Jr., 156
White, William Wesley, 156-57
White House, Brentsville, 95-96
Wigglesworth, Mrs., 18
Wilkins, Edmund, 142
Williams, Annie Thomas Henderson Kendall, 106-107
Williams, John, 95
Williams, Milton E., 106
Williams Ordinary, 19, 133
Williams Tract, 145
Wood, Ben, 88
Wood, Henry, 88
Wood, Wallace, 88
Woods Store, Greenwich, 88

About the Author

In the more than a quarter of a century in which she has lived in northern Virginia, D'Anne Evans has found looking into its history an endless fascination. In the past thirteen years she has been offered opportunities to write about it. Some of the results include *Wakefield Chapel*, done for the Fairfax County Office of Comprehensive Planning; the *Story of Oakton, Virginia* written for the Oakton Citizens Association; "Cooper Curtice: Soldier on the Quiet Frontier," an article published in *Medical Heritage*, which grew out of material from the Oakton study; and a series of articles on the Little River Turnpike. She received a bachelor of journalism degree from the University of Missouri at Columbia and a master's degree in history from Stanford University. Her interest in history has provided many pleasant and stimulating contacts with fellow historians. She is the current president of the Historical Society of Fairfax County, a past president of the Northern Virginia Association of Historians, and a charter member of Historic Prince William.

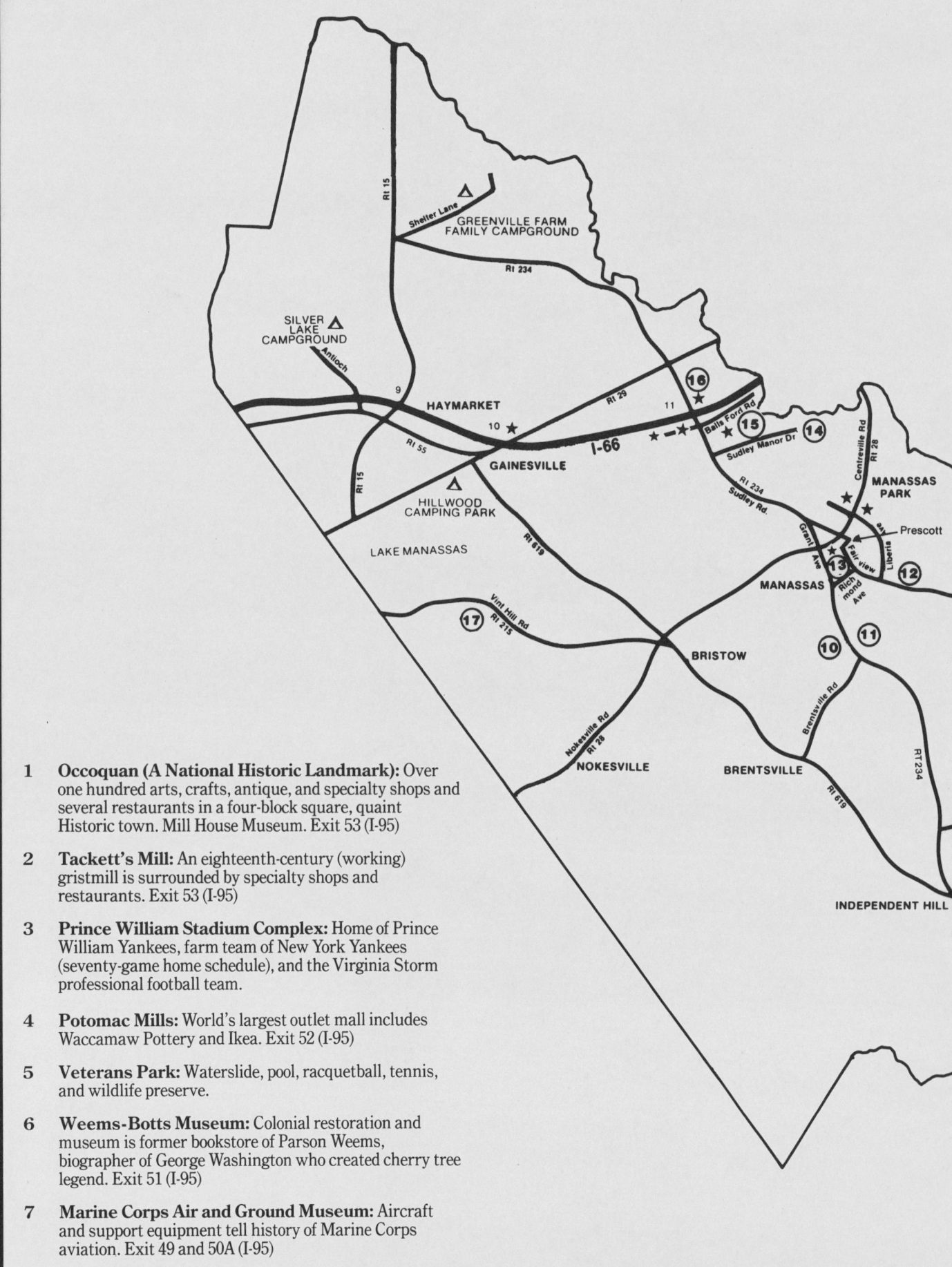

1. **Occoquan (A National Historic Landmark):** Over one hundred arts, crafts, antique, and specialty shops and several restaurants in a four-block square, quaint Historic town. Mill House Museum. Exit 53 (I-95)

2. **Tackett's Mill:** An eighteenth-century (working) gristmill is surrounded by specialty shops and restaurants. Exit 53 (I-95)

3. **Prince William Stadium Complex:** Home of Prince William Yankees, farm team of New York Yankees (seventy-game home schedule), and the Virginia Storm professional football team.

4. **Potomac Mills:** World's largest outlet mall includes Waccamaw Pottery and Ikea. Exit 52 (I-95)

5. **Veterans Park:** Waterslide, pool, racquetball, tennis, and wildlife preserve.

6. **Weems-Botts Museum:** Colonial restoration and museum is former bookstore of Parson Weems, biographer of George Washington who created cherry tree legend. Exit 51 (I-95)

7. **Marine Corps Air and Ground Museum:** Aircraft and support equipment tell history of Marine Corps aviation. Exit 49 and 50A (I-95)